THE LIFE AND TIMES OF

SHERLOCK HOLMES

THE LIFE AND TIMES OF
SHERLOCK HOLMES

PHILIP WELLER
WITH CHRISTOPHER RODEN

BRACKEN BOOKS
LONDON

First published 1992 by Studio Editions Ltd.,
Princess House, 50 Eastcastle Street, London W1N 7AP, England.

Copyright © Studio Editions Ltd., 1992

This edition published 1993 by Bracken Books,
an imprint of Studio Editions Ltd.

Designed and edited by Anness Publishing,
Boundary Row Studios,
1 Boundary Row, London SE1 8HP

Designer: Adrian Waddington
Watermark Communications Group Ltd.,
Chesham, England.

ISBN 1-85891-106-0

Printed and bound in Singapore

CONTENTS

PREFACE

It has reasonably been claimed that more foreign visitors to London know the address of Sherlock Holmes than know that of the Prime Minister: yet Sherlock Holmes never existed. The current occupants of Sherlock Holmes's famous address, the Abbey National bank, receive thousands of letters for Sherlock Holmes every year and have to employ a secretary to deal with his correspondence: yet Sherlock Holmes never existed. Respected pillars of society around the world spend countless hours examining every aspect of Sherlock Holmes's life: yet Sherlock Holmes never existed. What is the fascination which this apparently fictional character holds, and has held for many decades, for those who are his dedicated followers? No-one has ever produced a single, satisfactory answer to that question, but this book will attempt to explore the areas from which that fascination grows. The authors of this book invite you to join them in an exploration of the land where Sherlock Holmes still lives, a place where it is always 1895, and a place where, to paraphrase the words used by Holmes in calling Doctor John H. Watson to embark on yet another adventure:

"The Game Is Still Afoot."

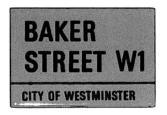

THE LIFE AND TIMES OF SHERLOCK HOLMES

THE LEGENDARY MR HOLMES

The Birth of the Great Detective

In 1882 a physician of Irish descent and Scottish birth set up his first independent practice in the genteel seaside resort of Southsea in Hampshire. The practice was slow to grow, and to while away the hours this young doctor began to develop his interest in the writing of adventure stories. During March and April of 1886 he produced a story with a completely new type of lead character: a private, consulting detective who produced amazing results through the application of a keen, analytical mind to the careful observation of the clues available. It was thus that Sherlock Holmes first saw the light of day, and the delivery was performed by Doctor Arthur Conan Doyle.

The first Holmesian appearance was in an adventure called *A Study in Scarlet*. This is one of the four Holmes long stories, and it was never to be a financial success for Doyle. He tried various publishers and received numerous rejections before he finally accepted the princely sum of £25, offered by Ward Lock, for the total rights to the story. Even then, the publishers managed to include an implied insult with their offer, in mentioning that: "We could not publish it this year as the market is flooded at present with cheap fiction . . ." The story appeared the following year, in November 1887, as part of a magazine called *Beeton's Christmas Annual*, produced by the brother of the more famous cookery book author. Doyle later remarked that he never received a further penny from the story, but such are

the changes in values that a mint copy of that one-shilling magazine would now sell for many tens of thousands of pounds, and the manuscripts of some of his shorter stories have sold for six-figure sums.

The Early Growth of Sherlock Holmes

A Study in Scarlet provided an excellent introduction to Sherlock Holmes and to his colleague and biographer Doctor Watson, as well as to the then revolutionary forensic

FIRST EDITION OF *A STUDY IN SCARLET* (above). *The book, published in 1888, was illustrated by Charles Altamont Doyle, the author's father.*

DR JOSEPH BELL (left), *Conan Doyle's professor of medicine at Edinburgh University and the original inspiration for the sleuth of Baker Street.*

WILLIAM GILLETTE AS SHERLOCK HOLMES (opposite). *Illustration of the renowned actor from a 1907 issue of* Vanity Fair. *The artist was Leslie Ward, better known as "Spy".*

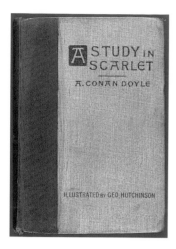

SECOND EDITION OF *A STUDY IN SCARLET*, 1891 *(above)*. *Illustrated by George Hutchinson.*

THE SIGN OF FOUR (right). The second edition, 1892.

THE SIGN OF THE FOUR (far right) was the second Holmes story to appear and was featured in Lippincott's Monthly Magazine, *February 1890.*

FIRST EDITION OF *THE ADVENTURES OF SHERLOCK HOLMES*, 1892 *(below). Illustrated by Sidney Paget.*

THE SIGN OF FOUR, 1902 *(below right). Souvenir edition.*

THE FIRST BOOK EDITION OF *THE SIGN OF FOUR*, 1890 *(below far right). Conan Doyle had the title shortened for the book.*

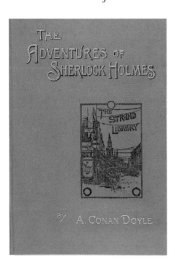

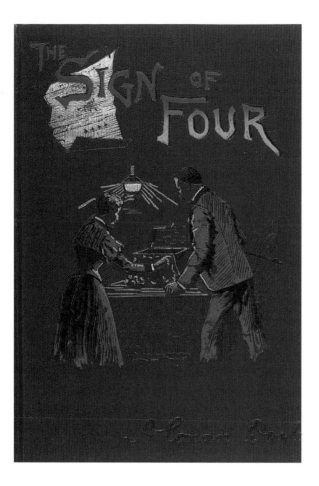

methodology which Holmes uses. This story was to form a good basis for those which followed, although it will be seen that some of the later stories include details which clash with those in the original narrative. The stories were never seen as great literature by Doyle, and his annoyance with his public's almost total preoccupation with Holmes later decided him to kill off the character. Initially, however, he saw the popularity of his new creation as a means towards being able to devote more time to "serious" writing.

In August 1889, at a dinner given by J.M. Stoddart, a literary agent for the American

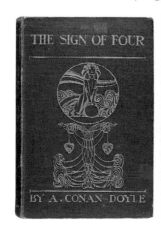

Lippincott's Monthly Magazine, Oscar Wilde and Conan Doyle were encouraged to produce new novels. The results were Oscar Wilde's famous *The Picture of Dorian Gray* and the second Holmes long story *The Sign of the Four*. The latter was the original title of the story, but Doyle shortly afterwards decided that he preferred the shorter title *The Sign of Four*, which is how it is usually known now. He produced the book in only six weeks.

Doyle moved from Southsea to central London in 1890 to specialize as an oculist, but this practice met with a similar lack of success and he found even more time for his writings. He began to produce the twelve immortal stories which were later combined as *The Adventures of Sherlock Holmes*, a volume containing many of the most popular of the short stories.

July 1891 saw the beginning of an extremely successful series of collaborations, with these new Holmes short stories being published in the monthly *The Strand Magazine* and accompanied by the illustrations of Sidney Paget. The commission for the illustrations was originally meant for Sidney's brother, Walter, but was mistakenly sent to

Sidney, who used Walter as his model. The Paget portraits were to fix the physical image of Holmes almost indelibly in the minds of many British readers. In America, however, the Holmesian image has been more closely associated with the later illustrations of Frederic Dorr Steele in *Collier's* magazine. From the often Samurai-like portraits of Holmes in many Japanese publications, it appears that Holmes is able to be all things to all nations.

The "Death" of Sherlock Holmes

In the summer of 1892, Doyle began producing the next thirteen short stories, twelve of which were later to become *The Memoirs of Sherlock Holmes*, for *The Strand Magazine*. Only a year later, however, he had already decided to end the life of the character he considered to be from "a lower stratum of literary achievement". In the Christmas 1893 issue of *The Strand Magazine*, the public was devastated to read of the death of Sherlock Holmes at the Reichenbach Falls in Switzerland, in *The Final Problem*. City gentlemen in London wore black armbands, and Doyle received threats and letters of abuse. In spite of his poor opinion of the Holmes stories, Doyle did take note of the feelings which others had for the character, but it was not until 1901 that he was to give way to pressures for more narratives about Holmes.

The initial result of Doyle's change of heart was the greatest of the long Holmes stories: a Holmes adventure from before his "demise", *The Hound of the Baskervilles*. It was here that the Holmes phenomenon reached an early peak, with queues forming outside the *Strand Magazine* offices in London on the monthly publication days. In America alone, the print run of the magazine was increased by nearly 200,000 copies.

WALTER PAGET AND SIDNEY PAGET *(left, above). Although Walter had been the intended illustrator for the* Strand *stories, the project was mistakenly sent to Sidney, who then modelled his illustrations of Holmes on his younger brother.*

REICHENBACH FALLS (*right*). *A late-Victorian colour print of the famous Swiss waterfall where Moriarty and Holmes had their final bout.*

LETTER TO DOYLE (*far right*), *1904, from a reader offering a housekeeper to assist the retired Sherlock Holmes.*

ARTHUR WONTNER AND LYN HARDING *portraying Holmes and Moriarty in the 1935 British film* The Triumph of Sherlock Holmes.

The Return from Reichenbach

In 1903, the event which all Holmesians had hoped for occurred, when Doyle was offered the then record sum of $45,000 by *Collier's* to produce thirteen new short Holmes stories. Sherlock Holmes rose from a watery grave, which was shown to have never existed, in *The Empty House*. These stories were later collected as *The Return of Sherlock Holmes*, but many enthusiasts considered that the resurrected Holmes was never as good as he had been. (This was, perhaps, an early example of something familiar to modern followers of long-running television programmes – the "third-series syndrome", where the plots become more mechanical and repetitive and the characters lack fresh development!) The collection does, however, contain some great stories.

A further series of adventures began their individual publication in 1908 with *Wisteria Lodge*. This collection of eight stories, known as *His Last Bow*, did not appear until 1917, with the last of the four Holmes long stories, *The Valley of Fear*, intervening in 1914–15. The collection included *The Cardboard Box*, an older story which Doyle had suppressed from his collected publication at the time of *The Memoirs*. The final collection of Holmes short stories, which began individual publication in 1921, was issued as *The Case-Book of Sherlock Holmes* in 1927, and many of these stories are definitely considered to be of inferior quality. The last story to be written was *Shoscombe Old Place*, although chronologically it takes place before Holmes's final adventure, which is *His Last Bow*.

The Sherlock Holmes Phenomenon

With the death of Sir Arthur Conan Doyle in 1930 the full range of Sherlock Holmes narratives was four long stories and 56 short stories: these stories have become known as the Sherlock Holmes Canon, or more simply as the 'Canon'. There are some additional pieces by Doyle which contain Holmes as a character, such as a very short story written to be produced as a miniature book for the royal doll's house at Windsor, and some references to an amateur consulting detective in other Doylean stories, such as *The Man with the Watches* and *The Lost Special*, but the world's continuing demand for Holmes stories has otherwise had to be met, with enormously varying degrees of success, by the many authors who have since produced pastiches and parodies about the "Master" and adaptations of the original stories.

Public demand for Holmesian adventures has also been met by the worlds of theatre, film and television. Perhaps the most popular stage actor to portray Holmes was William Gillette, whose 1899 play *Sherlock Holmes* was a massive success in America and, later, in England. This play introduced

THE SAINTSBURY PIPE *(above). This specially sculpted pipe, a portrait of the actor H.A. Saintsbury, was presented to him by his producer, Charles Frohman, on the occasion of Saintsbury's 500th performance as Sherlock Holmes on 21st December, 1903.*

WILLIAM GILLETTE AS HOLMES *(left above) surrounded by some of the other characters represented in the Canon.*

SHERLOCK HOLMES STARRING WILLIAM GILLETTE *(left and below) from the 1916 film based on his long running play. In the scene of the arrest of Moriarty, Gillette is pictured second from the right. Below, the actress Marjorie Kay portrays Alice Faulkner, Holmes's erstwhile love interest in the stage version. Gillette based Alice Faulkner on Irene Adler from* A Scandal in Bohemia.

WILLIAM GILLETTE (*above*) *as he appeared in his stage play* Sherlock Holmes, *1900. Gillette was famous for his portrayal of the great detective on both sides of the Atlantic.*

EILLE NORWOOD (*right above*) *in the play* The Return of Sherlock Holmes, *1923. He was best known for his screen appearances as the master sleuth, portraying Holmes in 47 silent films.*

BASIL RATHBONE *became Hollywood's most famous Holmes, yet the 1953 version of the play* Sherlock Holmes (*below*) *by Ouida Rathbone, the actor's wife, lasted for only three performances. His earlier portrayals of the detective, as in* The Adventures of Sherlock Holmes (*right*), *with Nigel Bruce as Watson, 1939, were more enduring.*

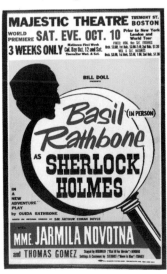

the public to one of the most famous Holmesian accoutrements, the curved pipe, an object not specifically mentioned in the stories, which Gillette used primarily because he could not speak his lines with a straight pipe in his mouth.

More films have been made about Sherlock Holmes than about any other character in the literature of the whole world, with one actor, Eille Norwood, appearing in 47 different Holmes films. Arthur Wontner gave an interesting interpretation of Holmes in the thirties, although many considered him to be too old for the part. In the forties, Basil Rathbone rapidly became identified as the archetypal screen Holmes of his time, although few of the scripts of his fourteen Holmes films had any connection with the Doylean Canon. Unfortunately, Rathbone's Watson, Nigel Bruce, was forced to play his part as a bumbling fool, which did a great and lasting disservice to the more intelligent and subtle original.

More accurate film renditions of Watson have since appeared, with André Morell in *The Hound of the Baskervilles* and with James Mason's particularly sympathetic version alongside Christopher Plummer's Holmes in the non-Canonical *Murder by Decree*.

Television has been a singularly effective medium for Holmes. Louis Hector was in fact the first TV Holmes, in a field test broadcasting of *The Three Garridebs* which appeared months before the official commencement of TV services in the USA, in 1937. Douglas Wilmer and Peter Cushing starred in important Holmesian series for British television in the late sixties, which better revealed the potential for Holmes on the small screen. In the late eighties and early nineties, Granada TV in Britain devoted a great deal of research and resources to producing what has certainly been seen as the definitive Holmesian series of the period, with Jeremy Brett providing a finely studied if occasionally over-mannered representation of Holmes. Much of the success of the series has come from the excellent performances of David Burke and, latterly, of Edward Hardwicke as Watson, for the importance of this character is often under-emphasized in the visual adaptations of the Canon, where Watson's fine descriptive powers are no longer an essential requirement.

The Future

The centenary of the first Holmes story, in 1987, saw celebrations around the world, and a massive increase in interest in all matters connected with Holmes. It seems that this interest will continue to grow as each generation finds something new to meet their own requirements in that Holmesian world which is ever the same, yet always new.

MICHAEL CAINE *(below) as an unconventional, bumbling Holmes in a publicity still from the film* Without A Clue.

JAPANESE PROGRAMME FOR *SHERLOCK'S LAST CASE (left). Charles Marowitz's play appeared in Japan in September 1988. The appeal of Baker Street is international and in Japan Holmes has one of the largest popular followings anywhere in the world.*

JEREMY BRETT *(far left) portrayed the detective in Granada Television's production of* The Hound of the Baskervilles, *as well as the successful series.*

SHERLOCK HOLMES AND HIS TIMES

The Holmesian Era

"Good old Watson! You are the one fixed point in a changing age." These words are part of Holmes's last speech in his final case, *His Last Bow*, and they show that Holmes was very much aware of the many changes which had occurred during his active life as a detective, which was in turn a reflection of the social awareness of his creator, Doyle. The unique nature of Holmes is revealed not only by the fact that he was born five years before his creator, in 1854, but by the supposition that he is still "alive" in 1992, sixty-two years after the death of his literary parent. Holmes's life has therefore spanned six reigns, two world wars and an almost total social revolution in the country of his birth. In considering Holmes in his most famous role, however, we must confine ourselves primarily to those years when he was active as a consulting detective. His first case was *The "Gloria Scott"* in 1873, and although he retired in late 1903 or early 1904, after *The Creeping Man*, he returned to serve his country prior to the outbreak of the First World War in *His Last Bow*; in all, a span of some 40 years during which Britain underwent considerable change.

Holmes's Education

Holmes describes himself as being the descendant of country squires and a grandson of a sister of the French artist Vernet (*The Greek Interpreter*). It is not recorded where he was born, although many supporters favour North Yorkshire, partly because of a house called "Mycroft" located on the moors. This author considers Derbyshire to be a strong contender, because of the presence of a branch of the Holmes family living in the vicinity of the Duke of Holdernesse, and because of Sherlock's very personally antagonistic attitude to that Duke during his visit to the Peak District in *The Priory School*.

Any form of education, beyond the most elementary, had to be paid for at that time,

OTTO LAGONI, *starring in a very loose interpretation of the detective of Baker Street in* The Confidence Trick, *a Danish film of 1910.*

PETER CUSHING *(opposite) as Holmes in a publicity still for the Hammer Films production of* The Hound of the Baskervilles, *1959.*

THE BOOKS AND JOURNALS IN HOLMES'S STUDY, *as featured in the Sherlock Holmes Pub in London. The pub has meticulously recreated the eclectic surroundings of the famous detective of 221B Baker Street.*

ledge which Watson describes so well in *A Study in Scarlet*. Sherlock must, however, have received a more than rudimentary education, since he did spend at least two years at a university (The *"Gloria Scott"*). Again, financial constraints, combined with Sherlock's natural propensities, may have resulted in his studying at one of the less socially prestigious universities, with Manchester being a likely contender in terms of curriculum and proximity to areas such as Derbyshire and Yorkshire, although the Canon does suggest that Holmes had at least some acquaintance with Oxford or Cambridge (see page 100).

either through a tutor or at preparatory and public schools (one should be aware that an English "public" school is in fact a private school, often involving boarding residence for pupils). Sherlock's elder brother, Mycroft, obviously received a sound, socially acceptable education, probably at one of the better public schools and then Oxford or Cambridge, for him subsequently to have become such an influential figure in the corridors of governmental power. There may have been some financial difficulties in providing a second son with a similar level of education, and this could perhaps help to explain Sherlock's lack of the sort of conformity which was bred at the public schools of that time, as well as the gaps in Sherlock's general know-

The Young Sleuth

Holmes was obviously not financially comfortable when he moved to London in 1874. Although the few cases which were brought to him by his college acquaintances helped him to pursue the specialist knowledge which he needed to become better able to deal with his later cases, he probably required some small assistance from his family to survive. When he first met Watson in 1881, he did so because he had informed Stamford that he needed someone to share the costs of the rooms which he had found at 221B Baker Street. Watson records that even in their earliest days together Holmes was visited by many peculiar characters, providing him with information or seeking

OLD BAKER STREET *as it appeared when Holmes and Watson made their home and solved so many crimes there.*

advice. Amongst the latter was Inspector Lestrade of Scotland Yard, and we must examine later Holmes's relationships with the official police.

In class-ridden Victorian society, Holmes appears to have been at ease with every level of that society, and he was not afraid to be openly critical of even the most highly-born of his clients, as with the King of Bohemia (*A Scandal in Bohemia*). There are suggestions of a resentment of social privilege in Holmes's attitudes, and this has even been taken to have been the product of some illicit relationship between a member of the nobility and a member of the Holmes family, a far from uncommon occurrence in British society at that time. A very explicit example of this is recorded in connection with John Clay in *The Red-Headed League*.

Holmes's often-mentioned drug abuse occurs primarily in the early part of his career, although there are indications that the temptations continue later, but this would have been seen as a less serious problem than it is now. Many strong drugs were then in common use, with laudanum, an alcoholic tincture of opium, still being available for quietening fractious infants. Many respectable physicians were regularly

experimenting with drugs which are now realized to be potentially very dangerous, with Doyle carrying out such experiments on himself at one stage in his career.

As Holmes became busier, the time available for his study of the new technologies for investigation of crime decreased, and the "missing three years" following the Reichenbach incident in 1891 must have provided an excellent opportunity for Holmes to progress with researches such as those he carried out on coal-tar derivatives in Montpellier (*The Empty House*). He also broadened his understanding of many other aspects of the world and its ways, whilst visiting such almost inaccessible rulers as the Dalai Lama in Tibet and the Khalifa at Khartoum. His report to the Foreign Office on the latter visit must have established his potential for useful work in a later age, in more complicated international negotiations. The contacts Holmes must have made during his residence in France in that period may also have been helpful between the two wars, especially in the early 1920s when diplomatic differences arose between England and France.

Holmes's Later Career

Holmes's many successes, and the publicity given to them by Watson, certainly served a most useful function for Holmes in bringing him even more interesting cases. He appears to have had a general disinterest in monetary matters, although those cases

SCIENCE OF SLEUTHING *(above left).* The Radio Times, *in celebration of the centenary of* A Study in Scarlet, *published this article dedicated to the mastery and intrigue of Sherlock Holmes.*

BAKER STREET *(above) in the mid-1890s, looking towards Marylebone Road. The busy street scene is typical of what Holmes would have seen when he ventured out of 221B.*

CLUTTERED CORNER OF HOLMES'S STUDY *(left) complete with various walking sticks for many of the detective's disguises, and chemicals that were used, among other things, for forensic experiments when analyzing clues.*

INTERIOR VIEWS OF HOLMES'S STUDY. *The Sherlock Holmes Pub has painstakingly recreated the study of 221B Baker Street, including artefacts relevant to many of the cases in the Canon. Notice the picture of Irene Adler on the mantelpiece (above right) and the harpoon used on a pig in* The Adventure of Black Peter.

which did pay well must have left him very comfortably provided for, as is shown by the high rent which Watson says that Holmes paid over the years for his rooms in Baker Street (*The Dying Detective*). He was also able to pay a high price, through the agency of his distant relative, Doctor Verner, for Watson's Kensington practice when Watson moved back in with Holmes after his return from his post-Reichenbach travels (*The Norwood Builder*). Perhaps his greatest mark of success was his audience with "a certain gracious lady" in 1895, and her presentation to him of a remarkably fine emerald tie-pin (*The Bruce-Partington Plans*). It is significant that Holmes never received any official rewards for his services, particularly as his brother Mycroft had suggested that these were available, and this again indicates Holmes's indifference, or disdain even, for the formal recognitions of Victorian life.

It also appears strange that at the age of only 50, seemingly at the peak of his career, Holmes retired. More so than Watson, he perhaps realized that the world was rapidly changing, and the new world may have been less to his tastes. Like his literary creator, he may well have been disgusted with the nature of man and his politics, as revealed through the disasters, disgraces and sheer inhumanity of the Boer War. It may, however, have been an increasing sense of boredom with the lack of originality in the cases which were being brought to him, for there are only a limited number of possibilities for originality in crime, and Holmes must have experienced most of them. Indeed it needed a threat to the safety of his country to bring him fully out of retirement for his final case.

The tensions which had built up in Europe between Holmes's retirement in 1903–4 and his temporary return to service in 1914 are very apparent in the conclusion of *His Last Bow*. Holmes had spent the early part of his retirement on the South Downs, where he kept bees, read philosophy and began writing the definitive study of detection, although his peaceful way of life was disturbed by the arrival of crime at his own door in *The Lion's Mane*. He was to return to this quiet solitude during and after the First World War, but it does seem to be almost unthinkable that he has not become involved in the momentous events which have occurred since 1914. Perhaps, as Watson has been busy elsewhere, any exploits which have involved Holmes have not been so dramatically or publicly recorded.

In addition, the nature of the investigations carried out by Holmes have tended to reflect the times in which he has lived, and as any more recent cases involving Holmes may well have been more far-reaching in their consequences, Holmes may increasingly have had to emulate his elder brother by becoming the silent adviser of those who need his great abilities. Scotland Yard today uses a computer system known as HOLMES (Home Office Large Major Enquiry Service) to assist them in solving crimes. One cannot but help wonder whether this is merely a front, and that a certain unlisted telephone number in the South of England is actually very well known to a few of the descendants of Inspector Lestrade.

Holmes and "a Bad Lot"

Holmes inevitably interacted with the official force on many occasions, and they are generally shown to be inefficient if not actually incompetent in contrast with him. There had been numerous attempts at improving the policing of the nation, but a regularized force was not established until 1829, when the Metropolitan Police were introduced by Sir Robert Peel. It was from their founder's name that policemen were to be known as "Bobbies" and "Peelers". The headquarters of this force was at Scotland Yard in Westminster. A specialized

"BOBBIES". *Fashion in Britain changed drastically from the Victorian era to the 1930s for all but the Metropolitan police. The policeman of 1934 (left) wore a uniform virtually identical to that of his Victorian predecessor (below). The latter has a Bull's-eye lantern on his belt.*

Detective Department was set up in 1842, with only two detectives, and this strength had risen to only fifteen by 1868. Corruption became rife in this department, and following the so-called "Trial of the Detectives" in 1877, the department was largely

METROPOLITAN POLICE WAGON *from the late 19th century (below left). The wagons were used for mass arrests during large riots like those of "Bloody Sunday".*

SIR EDWARD BRADFORD
(below), *Commissioner of the*
Metropolitan Police, during
the final years that Inspector
Lestrade worked with Holmes.

[SCOTLAND-YARD, THE HEAD-QUARTERS OF THE METROPOLITAN POLICE.]

SCOTLAND YARD. *New*
Scotland Yard (above) became
the headquarters of the
Metropolitan Police in 1890
after a terrorist bomb
damaged the original
building (above right).

The CID had no powers outside of the Metropolitan districts of London, but they could be requested to provide help by the chief constable of another force. This procedure does not appear to have been followed when Holmes invited Lestrade to travel down to Dartmoor to assist with the conclusion of the Baskerville murder case. Holmes was correct, however, when he mentioned that Lestrade had been retained by the friends of James McCarthy to work on the case in the latter's favour in *The Boscombe Valley Mystery*, since the 1839 Metropolitan Police Act did allow private groups and individuals to hire policemen, provided that the full costs were borne by such people. This may give an entirely new meaning to the Holmesian phrase "engage a special", but it may also explain how Holmes was able to call in Lestrade for the Baskerville case.

There was a general discontent with conditions in the police, and these did not begin to improve until a new commissioner was appointed in 1890. Sir Edward Bradford visited all of his stations and soon put right many of the grievances. He also introduced a newspaper, known as *The Police Gazette*, and although this was only intended for police forces it would have provided an excellent source of information for Holmes, who no doubt arranged to obtain regular copies through one of his police contacts.

re-staffed and reorganized as the Criminal Investigation Department (CID) in 1878. Lestrade and Gregson, who were described as being "the pick of a bad lot" by Holmes in 1881, may have cleanly survived the 1877 trial, for Lestrade certainly remarked that he had more than twenty years' experience in *A Study in Scarlet*. In a terrorist bombing attack in 1884, the CID offices were almost destroyed, and the headquarters moved to new premises at New Scotland Yard on the Embankment in 1890.

24

The reforms at Scotland Yard also extended into the fields of scientific detection, and many of the methods of Sherlock Holmes became the basis for developments in forensic science. Holmes's careful observation and recording of the scene of a crime became a standard procedure with the CID, as did Doyle's suggested use of plaster casts of foot impressions. Holmes does make several references to finger and thumb marks in solving some of his cases, but the use of fingerprints as a means of uniquely identifying individuals was not adopted by Scotland Yard until 1901.

The 1880s saw a great deal of social unrest in Britain, much of it associated with an economic depression, but also with problems such as the unpopularity of the monarchy resulting from the Queen's withdrawal from public affairs after the death of her beloved Prince Albert. There was also an increase in sexually orientated crimes, and with this came an increasing popularization of discussions of the psychological causes of such problems, although some have claimed that the relationship may have been partially the other way around. Holmes himself made attempts to reconstruct crimes from the viewpoint of the criminal, and this too became a standard practice of detection. It is also significant that when Watson first meets Holmes, the latter has just developed an infallible means of chemically identifying blood stains. Once again this reflects not only Holmes's advanced procedures, but Doyle's own wide interests and his attempts at making both the public and officialdom aware of the potentials of new sciences and methodologies. Holmes was also aware of longer-term trends in crime, and he frequently quotes previous cases from his in-

dexes where similar methods had been used before. This was an approach that was to be fully developed by the official force through the Criminal Records Office, with the result that the repeated use of a particular *modus operandi* by a criminal has often resulted in his or her downfall.

A general decrease in the crime rate during the 1890s allowed the establishment of better relationships between the police and the public, as well as time for the further development of improved methods of policing and crime detection. Although Holmes was generally disparaging about the police in his early career, he does suggest that in this later period they led the world in thoroughness and method (*The Three Garridebs*). One area in which there still appears to have been a problem was that of class. Lestrade is described as being an inspector in 1881, and he may have held that rank for some time by then. Although Holmes frequently points to Lestrade's ineptitude, it is Lestrade who is given the credit for solving many of Holmes's cases, as far as the authorities were concerned. In spite of this apparent success he is still an

"BLOODY SUNDAY" *(above). The workers' riot of 1887 in London.*

BERTILLON INSTRUMENTS *(right below) for measuring bone size. This was one standard method of criminal identification used by the Metropolitan police in the late-Victorian era.*

"AN ARREST" *(left below).*

ORIGINAL HANDCUFFS AND TRUNCHEON *(below) as used by the first "Bobbies".*

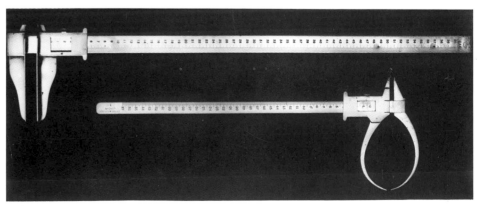

inspector in 1895. Perhaps the relationship between Sherlock Holmes and the police can best be summarized in an alleged incident in the life of the creator. When Doyle arrived in Egypt in 1895 he supposedly found that the Sherlock Holmes stories had been translated into Arabic and issued to the local police as a textbook!

Holmes and Crime

The Victorian public was fascinated by sensational crime, and the press eagerly satisfied that fascination. Holmes himself is described by Watson as having an immense knowledge of sensational literature. There do seem to have been fashions in crime,

THE WHITECHAPEL HORRORS. *The most celebrated serial murder cases of late-Victorian London. The speculation over the true identity of the infamous Jack the Ripper continues to this day while the questions of cover-up grow. Yet perhaps the most intriguing question is why wasn't Sherlock Holmes consulted?*

probably as a result of imitations of some of the more lurid crimes given coverage by the newspapers. There was a great popularity in late-Victorian London for dismembering murder victims and distributing the parts around the city. One particularly audacious murderer travelled by omnibus, carrying the head of his victim wrapped in a napkin on his knees. It is probably apocryphal, however, that he almost gave himself away by paying double after asking the fare and being told that it was "sixpence a head"!

Much of the crime of the time was, however, less grotesque, although of a nature which was particularly abhorrent to the middle and upper classes of Victorian society, being crimes against property. As with many other aspects of Victorian morals, there was an ambivalence between the supposed public attitudes to crime and actual private, individual attitudes. At the end of the century Doyle's brother-in-law, E.W. Hornung, began to produce a series of stories about an upper-class gentleman-criminal called Raffles, a character who quickly caught the admiration of a wide audience. Holmes himself was not averse to committing such crimes as burglary in the pursuit of those he suspected, and he occasionally acted as his own court of law in deciding whether those he discovered to be criminally guilty should be brought before the official courts.

The question must, almost inevitably, be asked as to why Holmes does not appear to have been called in to assist the police with the most notorious crime of the age, the "Jack the Ripper" murders which occurred in 1888. It does seem unlikely that Holmes would not have involved himself in the investigation, even if he was not consulted officially, and it would seem equally unlikely that – being who he was – he would not have found the criminal, or criminals, involved. Thus it is possible that he did just this, and that there was no subsequent public recognition of the fact because of some political, high-society or simple police embarrassment involved in the solving of the notorious crime. It certainly seems strange that the hundreds of extra policemen drafted into the Whitechapel district were all suddenly withdrawn shortly after the last murder, when no culprit had been found. It is a fact that the Metropolitan

Police commissioner of that time deliberately interfered with some of the evidence, and that he was later forced to resign in the face of public allegations of incompetence. It is also true that the Scotland Yard documents relating to the crime were closed to public inspection for many decades, and that some of those documents are now missing. Perhaps those missing documents revealed not only the criminal but also that a certain consulting detective had been foremost in discovering his identity. (See page 45 for another possible view.)

Sherlock Holmes and Communications

Holmes's methodology required a constant availability of accurate and current information. Much of this he obtained from newspapers, which helped to maintain his own meticuously filed index system, although he did inform Watson that his reading of such periodicals was restricted to the crime reports and the agony columns. Holmes had a very wide choice of reading available to him, with sixteen different London newspapers being mentioned in the Canon in addition to the many provincial news sources. His belief that the ability to identify different newspapers from the typeface they used and the quality of materials was "one of the most elementary branches of knowledge to the special expert in crime" is stated in *The Hound of the Baskervilles*, and this was yet another area where the official police were to follow his lead.

MAGNETO WALL TELEPHONE *(above). When not sending telegraphs or posting letters the modern Magneto is certainly the method of urgent communication Holmes would have used in his later cases.*

HOLMES'S LOCAL LETTER BOX *(left). Removed in 1963, this letter box on Chiltern Street was the nearest to what would have been 221B Baker Street and the one most likely used by Holmes and Watson.*

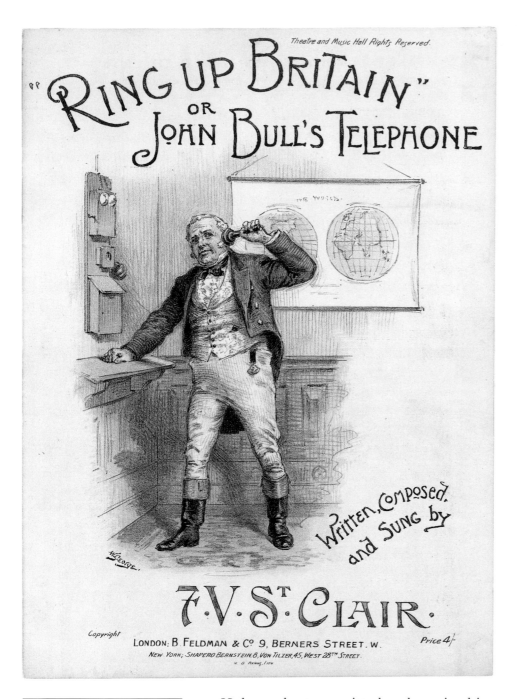

EDWARDIAN SONG SHEET. *Despite the telephone's popularity in the early 1880s, it is doubtful that Holmes would have ever attempted the tune "Ring Up Britain" on his violin.*

Holmes also transmitted and received information by letter, and here he had a far better national service than is now available, with up to a dozen deliveries of mail each day. It was commonplace in London to post a letter in the morning and receive the reply in the afternoon of the same day, and even on Dartmoor the letters which Watson sent to Baker Street were delayed by only a day before reaching Holmes back on Dartmoor. In addition to this, a more direct mail and parcel delivery service was possible through agencies such as the district messenger services, albeit at twice the Post Office rates. Holmes thoroughly trusted the reliability of such services, remarking that only murder would stop the messenger boys from making their deliveries (*The Six Napoleons*).

For even more rapid communications, however, Holmes's favourite medium was the telegram, as Watson attests when he remarks that Holmes had never been known to write where a telegram would serve (*The Devil's Foot*). The first public telegraph system had been opened in 1843, covering the twenty miles between Paddington and Slough, and within two years its potential for police work was revealed when a suspected murderer, John Tawell, was arrested at Paddington after a message had been passed from Slough when the suspect boarded a train there. As the telegraph system did not include the letter "Q" in its alphabet, Tawell was described as being "in the garb of a Kwaker", and this rendition of Quaker was sufficiently understood for him to be identified. The telegram did have the obvious disadvantage of needing a telegraph office for the message to be sent, as this could often be at many miles' distance from a particular location, as with the Grimpen Post Office for Baskerville Hall, but it was almost worth having the telegraph invented to allow Holmes the imperiousness with which he summoned Watson by telegram with "Come at once if convenient – if inconvenient come all the same. S.H." (*The Creeping Man*).

For once Scotland Yard does seem to have been in advance of Holmes in the employment of one of the most convenient forms of communication, the telephone. Inspector Athelney Jones suggested telephoning the Yard in 1888 (*The Sign of Four*), whereas the first reference to a telephone at 221B Baker Street occurs ten years later (*The Retired Colourman*). The telephone certainly must have become essential for contacting Holmes once he retired to his house on the South Downs.

How Holmes Travelled

Holmes's journeys around London are almost inevitably associated with the hansom cab. These two-wheelers were a rapid and exhilarating form of transport, but one that was also noisy, uncomfortable and constantly in danger of overturning. Holmes does use many other forms of carriage, with

HOLMES AND WATSON
HAILING A HANSOM CAB.
A Paget illustration for
The Adventure of the
Cardboard Box.

the four-wheeler brougham being far more conducive to a safe and comfortable journey. It should be noted that when Watson (*The Dying Detective*) and Holmes (*The Final Problem*) whistle for a cab, they are not engaged in any vulgar practices involving the fingers being placed in the mouth, as Victorian gentlemen usually carried a special high-pitched cab whistle, with one blast summoning a four-wheeler and two a hansom. A cab journey across London would have been at around the same speed as today, as the traffic was almost as heavy, although the streets were far dirtier, with the deposits from the horses often only being removable at night. It is only in 1914, in Holmes's final recorded case (*His Last Bow*) that the motor car intrudes on the scene. Perhaps it is relevant that the then 62-year-old man about town, Watson, has learned to drive, whereas Holmes more fittingly remains part of the horse-drawn age for short journeys.

The underground railway did provide a more rapid method of transit in London, with the first line, the Metropolitan Railway, opening in 1863 to provide a three-and-a-half mile journey from Baker Street. In its first year this line carried over nine million passengers, which demonstrates the already-crowded nature of the city and its transport systems. This line, typical of the early lines, was very dirty, as the trains were steam-hauled. The first electric underground railway line did not open until 1896.

Holmes's journeys to the provinces and beyond were made primarily by railway, and he once again had a far better service available to him in many ways. Prior to 1923, Britain's railways were owned by hundreds of independent companies, and most of these were small branch-line companies feeding passengers to the main-line company routes all over the country. Competition between main-line companies often

TRAVELLING BY RAIL. *Holmes and Watson take in the "sordid" view of London from their compartment. A Paget illustration for* The Naval Treaty.

resulted in journey times which were not much slower than today. On-board facilities were sometimes luxurious, although not always so, and Holmes's Inverness cape may often have been used for its proper purpose, with the shoulder cape being pulled over the head for warmth on some long, draughty journeys.

The intricacies of the railway connections needed on rail journeys would have required some dexterous use of that indispensable item for the rail traveller, *Bradshaw's Railway Guide*, which was published monthly in Victorian times. Even within one company's lines, frequent changes would often have to be made. Holmes's casual suggestion on Canterbury station that he and Watson would change their destination from Dover to Newhaven would actually have involved at least three changes of train on the London, Brighton and South Coast Railway Company's lines and

would have taken at least six hours to complete. Holmes's statement that they would reach Brussels that night, after leaving Canterbury at lunch-time, was a little optimistic.

Holmes obviously used sea ferries for his various trips to the Continent, and on his wider world travels to Tibet and America, but the only sea journey which he mentions specifically is that in *The Final Problem*, from Newhaven to Dieppe. Faster ships had been introduced on this route in 1875, with a golden guinea being placed by the ship's captain on the top of the engine room hatch of the *Paris II* for the fireman if the crossing was made in under five hours, though this timing was not achieved until 1888. However, by the time that Holmes made his crossing the record had been reduced to under three and a half hours – which compares well with the four hours taken today. Holmes will have been concentrating on other problems during the crossing, but

BULL'S-EYE LANTERN. *Referred to as a "dark lantern" in* Speckled Band, Red-Headed League, Bruce-Partington Plans, Charles Augustus Milverton, Six Napoleons, *and* The Sign of Four, *this early flashlight (below) was often used by Holmes when forced to search for clues or suspects at night. In an untypically authentic way Basil Rathbone (left), as Hollywood's Sherlock Holmes, illuminates the scene with a Bull's-eye lantern.*

Watson may have recalled an accident which had occurred on that route only four years previously, when the *Victoria* went aground in fog and was subsequently lost. Nineteen passengers were drowned when a lady's wrap caught in the ropes and upturned the lifeboat in which they were being lowered. The macabre nature of the accident was increased when the cargo of black crepe slowly floated out from the hold to cover the ship in a dark shroud. Although many see the late-Victorian period as a golden age for travel, it was clearly not without its perils.

31

THE WORLD OF SHERLOCK HOLMES

HOLMESIAN AND SHERLOCKIAN SOCIETIES

Holmesians and Sherlockians

Holmesians and Sherlockians are those who, to varying degrees, are involved in Canonical scholarship, the study of the Sherlock Holmes stories. One must, naturally, ask what the difference is between Holmesians and Sherlockians, and the best answer is probably that of the American scholar who suggested that British Sherlockians prefer to call themselves Holmesians, whereas American Holmesians prefer to be called Sherlockians. This difference is probably a reflection of national character, with the British being more formal in their use of surnames and the Americans demonstrating their general affability with the use of forenames. The British practice is Canonically more correct, since Victorian gentlemen would almost invariably use surnames between themselves, other than when addressing relatives. Only Mycroft ever calls Holmes "Sherlock", although Mr Sherman does rather impudently refer to Holmes as "Mr Sherlock" in *The Sign of Four*. Even Watson, always calls him Holmes, and, being British, this author chooses to follow the practice of that greater writer. Scholarly activities associated with Holmes are not, however, limited to these two nations, as there are followers of Holmes in almost every country of the world.

Sherlock Holmes Societies

The senior Sherlock Holmes society of the world is generally recognized as being "The Baker Street Irregulars" of the USA. This society was founded in 1934, and although it has a deliberately small membership, it does have hundreds of affiliated scion societies throughout the USA. The names of some of these scion societies are an entertainment in themselves, with "The Afghanistan Perceivers", "The Bruce-Partington Planners", "The Giant Rats of Sumatra", "The Inverness Capers" and "The Scion of the Four" to mention only a

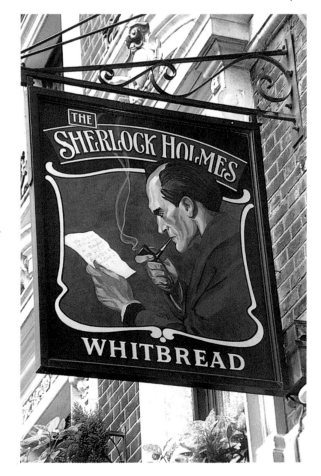

THE SHERLOCK HOLMES PUB *(above). An atmospheric view of the interior.*

SHERLOCK HOLMES PUB *(left). The sign, based on a Paget illustration, outside the pub near Charing Cross and Trafalgar Square. The pub is full of Holmesian memorabilia, including a finely reconstructed sitting room of 221B Baker Street. The pub is also of interest to Holmesian scholars because it used to be known as The Northumberland Hotel, which is where Sir Henry stayed when he first arrived in London (see* The Hound of the Baskervilles*).*

BASIL RATHBONE *as Sherlock Holmes, with briar pipe (opposite). A publicity still from the 1939 film* Adventures of Sherlock Holmes.

SHERLOCK HOLMES PUB. *The exterior of the pub (above right) is reproduced in a ceramic model (above).*

founded in 1951. One of the best-known activities of this society is their occasional re-creation of the famous fight between Holmes and Moriarty at the Reichenbach Falls in Switzerland, with over a hundred members in full Victorian costume present, each representing a character from the Canon. This large society does not have scion societies, but there are several independent regional Holmesian societies throughout Britain, ranging from "The Fratton Lodgers" in Holmes's literary birthplace of Portsmouth in the South to "The Northern Musgraves" in the North. A full

few. With some scholars claiming up to five wives for Watson, and with the repeated calls upon his time by Holmes, it is rather charming that there is also a scion society dedicated to the memory of "Doctor Watson's Neglected Patients". It is perhaps a little more surprising that there is a scion society called "The Brothers Three of Moriarty", although their true feelings are perhaps revealed by the fact that they hold an "Unhappy Birthday You Bastard Moriarty Celebration" each year, where buffalo droppings are added to a memorial pile!

In Britain the main society is "The Sherlock Holmes Society of London", which was

221B 1951 EXHIBITION. *The room was reconstructed for the Festival of Britain. It was in fact this exhibition which brought together many of the founders of what is today the Sherlock Holmes Society of London.*

register of independent British societies is maintained by "SHERLOCK" (Sherlock Holmes Enthusiasts Regionally Located Outside the Capital of the Kingdom).

Another major society in the world is "The Japan Sherlock Holmes Club", who were responsible for erecting the first life-size statue of Holmes. There are also smaller Japanese groups, such as "The Men with the Twisted Konjo"! Members of this society have paid homage to the Master at the Reichenbach Falls in traditional Samurai warrior costume, revealing the amazingly international appeal of Sherlock Holmes.

The above societies do accept members from other countries, but one truly international society is "The Franco-Midland Hardware Company", which is named after a fraudulent company set up in *The Stock-Broker's Clerk*, and which has its head office in England. This society provides a continuing correspondence study course on Sherlock Holmes, particularly aimed at those who are unable to attend the meetings of other societies, although it does also arrange its own meetings.

All of these societies, and those in other countries such as Australia, Canada, France, Germany and Spain are involved in similar activities: holding meetings with special lectures, discussions, quizzes and other amusements; publishing journals containing learned articles; and arranging expeditions to locations with Holmesian connections. Addresses are given on page 140 for contacting the main societies.

THE SITTING ROOM AT 221B *(above) the Sherlock Holmes Museum, Meiringen, Switzerland; (left) a 1968 reconstruction by Adrian Conan Doyle at his Swiss château.*

GERMAN FILM POSTER *for the Hollywood film* Terror By Night.

THE CASE OF THE SHERLOCK HOLMES SCHOLARS

"The Game"

In many of their activities, the members of the Holmesian societies are involved in what may be called "The Game", although some members would insist that their involvement was purely academic and serious in terms of literary and historical studies. In playing The Game, one has to accept the premise that Sherlock Holmes was, and still is, a real person, and that Doctor Watson is his real biographer. Sir Arthur Conan Doyle is relegated to the mere role of the "Literary Agent" for Watson, although all Holmesians do, of course, have a great respect and admiration for him outside of The Game.

Having accepted these premises, attempts are then made to examine every aspect of the Canon in terms of actual historical events and locations. This can to a large extent be done, because the stories were recorded with an excellent eye for the social history of the time and for real locations, although of course a great deal of licence is attributable to the Literary Agent in those recordings. One major consequence of this process is that a large number of problems are thereby revealed within the Canon. The true explanation of many of these problems is that the Literary Agent was not always scrupulous with such literary disciplines as continuity control, and that he often concentrated several separate locations into one small region to improve the dramatic quality of the story. This explanation cannot, however, be accepted when playing The Game. Dedicated Holmesians

also do not accept other, too-easy explanations, such as constantly attributing problems to Watson's notoriously bad memory, or to his habit of changing the facts to protect the innocent. A more interesting and challenging object for scholars is to explain the problems using only actual historical facts, the information contained in the Canon and good, logical arguments.

HOLMES AND MORIARTY *(above)*; *the statuette of Moriarty is modelled on the Paget illustration for* The Final Problem.

THE GREAT DETECTIVE *(left)*, *a ballet given by the Sadler's Wells Company in 1953, with Kenneth MacMillan as Holmes and Stanley Holden as Watson.*

HOLMES AND WATSON ON THE TRAIL OF THE HOUND *(opposite). Peter Cushing, right, and Andre Morell, left, in the 1959 Hammer Films production* The Hound of the Baskervilles.

"IT IS QUITE A THREE PIPE PROBLEM" *(above). Holmes is never described as specifically smoking a calabash in the Conan Doyle stories; however, he is usually portrayed puffing on one in film and on stage, as Michael Caine (middle, in* Without A Clue, *1989) and John Neville (right, in* A Study in Terror, *1965) demonstrate.*

VIGGO LARSEN LENDS AN EAR TO THE WOODWORK *(below) as Holmes in a 1909 Danish film from Nordisk,* Droske 519.

Some Problems in the Canon

One might begin at the beginning by attempting to determine when Sherlock Holmes was born. No date is given in the Canon, but in *His Last Bow*, which takes place in August 1914, he is described as being a man of 60. This may have been a generalization, but the birth year of 1854 does fit well with other indications in the Canon, and is generally accepted by scholars. The birth day is even less clearly indicated, but the date of 6th January is again generally accepted – partly on the grounds of Holmes's fondness for quoting from Shakespeare's *Twelfth Night* (or misquoting, as he does twice), and partly from indications in one case that a party may have taken place on the night before 7th January. Astrological analysis of Holmes's character, however, suggests that he is a Scorpio, with a birthday in November. It should perhaps be noted that the January date does allow Holmesians to celebrate his birthday in conjunction with New Year festivities!

It has been suggested that Holmes is still alive, which, in 1992, makes him 138 years old. This is possible because, the theory goes, following his escape from Reichenbach, Holmes travelled to Tibet, where he met the Dalai Lama and learned the secret of eternal life. He did finally retire in 1914, after *His Last Bow*, and he now lives on the South Downs, where he keeps bees, studies philosophy and is writing the definitive study on detection. He passed on the secret of eternal life to Watson, whose birth date has been calculated as being in 1852, extrapolated from the Canonical fact that he graduated from university in 1878.

Watson is supposed to be rather more actively engaged in his retirement. In *The Sign of Four*, Watson boasted that he had "an experience of women which extends over many nations and three separate continents", and he is currently travelling the remaining continents of the world to extend that knowledge further.

Holmes's early history is continued with considerations of which university he attended, with the primary contenders being Oxford and Cambridge. As with many other problems, the Canon itself provides only a few direct clues, and the remainder must be obtained from indirect evidence. In *The "Gloria Scott"*, Holmes mentions that he was at college for two years, and that he was bitten by the dog of a fellow student when on his way to chapel. Since college regulations in the 1870s banned dogs from the premises, it can be claimed that Holmes must have been bitten outside the college on his way into chapel. As Oxford students were in those days required to spend their first two years living in college, Holmes must have been at Cambridge, where students began with lodgings in the town. In *The Three Students*, however, Holmes refers to a quadrangle in a college, but quadrangles are known as courtyards at Cambridge, which suggests that he was an Oxford man. This is also suggested by his unfamiliarity with the Cambridgeshire countryside, and by his references to Cambridge as an inhospitable place, in *The Missing Three-Quarter*. Even the drawings of Sidney Paget are brought into the argument, when it is claimed that the hat band on Holmes's boater in *The "Gloria Scott"*, although drawn in black and white, appears to be light (blue), rather than dark (blue), thereby indicating Cambridge.

In 1988, The Sherlock Holmes Society of London spent their annual weekend expedition at Oxford proving conclusively that Holmes was an Oxford man. In 1989, the same society spent their annual expedition weekend in Cambridge, proving equally conclusively that he was a Cambridge man. The obvious conclusion from this might be that he attended both universities. Holmes's reference to spending two years at college would imply that he did not obtain a

degree, and this would agree with his habit of concentrating only on those elements of any subject which were of immediate use to him. This deliberation has not prevented other scholars from proposing Manchester or London universities as Holmes's alma mater, precisely because the subjects available at those universities would have been of more relevance to him. One scholar has even used evidence from the Canon to argue that Holmes must have attended Portsmouth Polytechnic, in spite of the fact that this institute was not founded until the 1960s. It should from this example alone be appreciated that Holmesian scholars do derive a great deal of fun, as well as more serious involvement, from their pastime.

Moving to an examination of Watson, it may be considered strange that a medical

HOLMES BRINGS HIS DEDUCTIVE SKILLS TO BEAR ON A HAT *in the 1965 film* A Study in Terror. *Billed as the "original caped crusader" in America, the dynamic duo of John Neville, as Holmes, and Donald Houston, as Watson, track down the notorious Jack the Ripper.*

A CAREFULLY BALANCED
BLEND OF 221B PIPE TOBACCO
MIXTURE *(below). Perhaps it
is the same blend of shag
tobacco Holmes enjoyed whilst
solving the case of* The Man
with the Twisted Lip?

man should suffer from the particular problem associated with him. On the very first page of the first Sherlock Holmes story, *A Study in Scarlet*, Doctor Watson informs us that he was wounded in the shoulder by a Jezail bullet at the Battle of Maiwand. Only a few years later, in *The Sign of Four*, he comments that he was wounded by a Jezail bullet in the leg. Investigations of "Watson's Wandering Wound" could fill several volumes of this size, but perhaps the best explanation is that his original, major wound was in the shoulder, and he was then wounded again, in the leg, as he was being evacuated from the battlefield. The varying intensity of the discomfort caused by these wounds would account for his different emphasis at different times. There are, however, still adherents of single-wound theories, who sometimes have to place the good doctor in some rather contorted positions to allow one bullet to wound both his shoulder and leg.

Medical considerations continue with an investigation of Holmes's drug abuse. Watson most graphically describes Holmes injecting himself with a seven-per-cent solution of cocaine in *The Sign of Four*, and there are other references to the use of morphine. Such references to drug abuse are primarily made in connection with Holmes's early career, and he explains his abuse on grounds of boredom with ordinary life. Watson later claims that he weaned Holmes off the habit, but it is much more likely that Holmes would simply have given up the habit when he became better known and thus received more interesting cases to deal with.

To return to Watson, there is a problem connected with his name. This is very clearly given by him as being John H. Watson, but nowhere in the Canon is it revealed what the "H" stands for. A problem connected with his first name occurs in *The Man with the Twisted Lip*, where his wife,

" 'DO YOU KNOW WHERE WE
ARE?' " *(far right), Holmes
asks Watson in* The Empty
House. *The two were
standing in Camden House,
the "Empty House", which
stands opposite 221B Baker
Street, photographed here in
1904.*

A POSSIBLE HOME FOR
HOLMES? *(right), the house in
Baker Street, photographed by
Dr Gray Chandler Briggs in
1921, claimed to be 221B.*

SECTION OF A LONDON STREET MAP *(above right) dating from 1870. Baker Street is located lower left.*

CHRISTOPHER LEE AS HOLMES. *The actor appeared as Holmes in the 1962 West German production* Sherlock Holmes and the Deadly Necklace *(above left). Needless to say, the costume got the thumbs down before it ever reached the film set.*

Mary, refers to him as James. It has been suggested that Mary would have had a natural dislike for the name John, because of its association with John Sholto, and that she might therefore have adopted a pet name for her husband. Dorothy L. Sayers suggested that this pet name was James as an anglicized version of Watson's middle name, Hamish, although others have since claimed that this is an incorrect translation.

It was mentioned in the Preface that almost everyone knows the address of Sherlock Holmes, yet this address itself becomes a major scholarship problem. During the period when Holmes was occupying his rooms in Baker Street, the numbers in that street reached only a two-figure level, and there was thus no number 221. The length of Baker Street has since been twice increased, firstly with the addition of the length of York Place and secondly with the length of Upper Baker Street. The current number 221 was originally in the latter of these streets. There are numerous descriptive clues in the Canon, although some of these, such as the reference to a plane tree in the back yard, may no longer be relevant. There should be seventeen steps between the ground floor and the first floor,

although this would have applied to many of the houses in the street and may also have been changed with time. Many clues are obtained from the description of the empty house opposite 221, "Camden House", and there are indirect indications as to the location, such as the fact that it appears to have been worthwhile catching a cab from Baker Street station to 221. The Literary Agent himself was somewhat evasive about the location, having on one occasion mentioned that he could not recall ever having been in Baker Street, although on another occasion he suggested that 221 was on the corner of George Street and Baker Street. This last suggestion shows the unreliability of the Literary Agent, since a corner site does not fit many of the requirements of the Canon. A general consensus is that the location is on the west side of Baker Street, somewhere between George Street and Crawford Street. This author's own preference is for number 31 Baker Street, but the original Victorian building no longer exists at that site.

The number of problems referred to above is only a small selection. There is space only for a minimal coverage of the evidence available and the possible solutions. Full volumes have been written on some of these problems, and there are many more which have not yet even been started on by scholars. For all those who are interested in playing The Game, the game is still very much afoot.

A SCHOLARLY CASE STUDY

*The Problem of Sherlock Holmes
and Jack the Ripper*
P.L. Anness

Lastly, and most controversially, we come to the greatest mystery in Holmes's career – on the principle of the dog that didn't bark – which is his apparent lack of involvement in the case of Jack the Ripper: the brutal slaying of five (or six, depending on the theory espoused) prostitutes in the East End of London between August and November in 1888. At this time Holmes was at his prime, and although he had not yet established his huge popular reputation, his work was well known and highly regarded in forensic circles, and he had already become the first point of call for the officials of Scotland Yard when they found themselves at a loss. It seems impossible, on the face of it, that he would not have been consulted on a matter which had so obviously baffled the authorities and which became, for a time, an issue which looked likely to destroy the nation's trust and belief in its police force – almost to the point of public disorder and riot.

A number of theories have been put forward to cover this omission. The commonly accepted explanation is that Holmes was involved in the case, and indeed solved it, but that the perpetrator was so positioned in the community – perhaps even of royal blood – that the detective was begged and persuaded not to reveal his findings for the good of the country. A second view, along the same lines, is that Holmes caught the criminal, but decided, again perhaps for political reasons, to take the matter into his own hands, and executed the killer himself rather than depending on the official mechanism.

Unfortunately there is a further theory, which, though abhorred by right-thinking people (including the authors of this volume), is included herein for the purposes of academic completeness. This is the hypothesis that Holmes himself was Jack the Ripper.

A profile of the Ripper was developed by the police at the time: necessarily primitive in those pre-Freudian days when neither the psychological nor the scientific fields of criminal investigation had reached any degree of sophistication. Essentially they were looking for a man who was almost certainly not a doctor, but who had some medical training or knowledge; someone who could move at will through the lowest sections of the community without drawing attention to himself; someone who could come and go as he pleased, with no parents, wife or friend living at home with him to observe his movements, demeanour, and condition; perhaps someone who had a knowledge of police procedures, so that he could anticipate and make counter moves against them; and certainly a man who had an antipathy towards women, who had perhaps been slighted or damaged by one, or who imagined some threat against himself from a female.

It is regrettable that Holmes fits the bill so precisely. Although not specifically trained in medicine, he took courses at the University of London Medical School, and his knowledge of anatomy is confessed by Watson to be "accurate, but unsystematic". Stamford, perhaps indicating something more sinister than was realized at the time, states that "he has amassed a lot of out-of-the-way knowledge which would astonish his professors". At the University he would have mixed with medical students, and had access (as he was allowed into the building without supervision) to equipment, tools, and, potentially, corpses. Remember, the evidence of Stamford is that he has seen Holmes experimenting on the "subjects" (donated bodies) in the dissecting room by beating them with a stick. He innocently accepts Holmes's explanation that he is investigating "how far bruises may be produced after death", but is this the truth? If it is, then it is not much more bizarre to suggest that the murders of the Whitechapel prostitutes may have been the grotesque scientific experiments of a diseased mind, unable any longer to differentiate between live and dead subjects.

Holmes's talent for disguise is well established. Due to the circumstances of the Ripper murders, no reliable descriptions were ever obtained. Those that were received were contradictory, implying that the murderer took some pains to change his appearance from time to time. Nothing would have been simpler for Holmes – often seen as a groom, a loafer, a seaman, and even a priest – to take on the guise of a person whose presence would have raised no comment in Whitechapel. There were even fantastic rumours at the time that the Ripper was a woman – and Holmes, as we know, could easily assume a female role.

Regarding his ability to come and go as he pleased, Holmes was, at this time, living alone at Baker Street, as Watson, having met Mary Morstan, was almost certainly living with his new wife. This is one of the most confusing aspects of the history. Watson had clearly become engaged following the *Sign of Four* case, which occured, we are told, "some years after" *A Study in Scarlet*, which we gather took place in March 1887. Yet in *A Scandal in Bohemia*, which is dated March 1888 (five months before the first Ripper killing), Watson states that "my marriage had drifted us away from each other" and that he was living away from Baker Street. This brings us to Watson's role in the affair. It was often suggested that the Ripper had a helper, but given our knowledge of the doctor's character we can hardly suspect him of any active role. On the other

hand somebody who lived so close to the man could not, realistically, have been totally absent of some suspicions, however mild or unformed. The confusion of the dates by Watson is consequently interpreted as an unconscious suppression of facts that may have implicated his friend. Regardless, it is very highly probable that Holmes was living alone at this time, and could therefore act unobserved. He had, in any case, the contacts in the East End, and the intelligence, to set up a sanctuary for himself there if he thought it advisable. Indeed, it has been pointed out that Holmes had only to inform the police that he was investigating the crimes, and he could have set himself up a temporary headquarters in the area and come and go as he pleased – he was uniquely above suspicion.

His knowledge of police procedure, and contempt for it, are legendary – he could easily have double-crossed Aberline, or any of the other officers on the case. Again, it has been suggested that his scorn for the authorities, and his almost obsessive desire to make them look foolish and show himself superior, may have been a key motivating factor in the crimes. His other characteristics – the sociopathic desire for instant gratification and fear of boredom; manic mood swings from frenetic activity to overwhelming lassitude; an obsessive fascination with crime and its processes; an intensely secretive nature, intermingled with an uncontrollable desire for publicity; a tendency towards drug-taking; and a superiority complex which on innumerable occasions allowed Holmes to place himself above the law as a determiner of justice – complement the picture of the typical serial-killer.

The principal motivating factor, and the last item in the police profile, was obviously a hatred of, or contempt for, women. Unfortunately Holmes again falls under suspicion. Although Watson normally – perhaps, once more, unconsciously protecting his friend – describes Holmes's misogyny as a simple lack of interest, it is not difficult, reading between the lines, to develop a more sinister interpretation. One wonders what was really said when Holmes is reported, on hearing of his friend's engagement: "I really cannot congratulate you . . . love is an emotional thing, and whatever is emotional is opposed to that true cold

THE ILLUSTRATED POLICE NEWS (opposite), 1888, brilliantly catered to the Victorian's insatiable appetite for murder, mutilation and all things morbid. What sort of mind could have committed such crimes? Did the murderer reside in Baker Street? Why wasn't Holmes contacted? It is interesting to note that, like "The Mysterious Monster of the East-End", the perpetrator of "The Whitehall Mystery" (lower strip) was never apprehended.

reason which I place above all things. I should never marry myself, lest I bias my judgement." More ominously, he is described by Watson in *A Scandal in Bohemia* in the following terms: "as a lover he would have placed himself in a false position. He never spoke of the softer passions, save with a gibe and a sneer."

The report by Watson entitled *A Scandal in Bohemia* is particularly important to the Holmes-as-Ripper theory. It has been noted that it dates from March 1888, shortly before the Ripper killings began, and that it opens with the barely veiled admission of

Holmes's mental hatred of women at the time. There is every probability that this hatred had been fostered by Watson's marriage and desertion. Without commenting on Holmes's sexuality, if wc review the events of the previous two years in his life, we can see what a shock Watson's departure from Baker Street would have caused in an already sensitive mind. We know that Holmes was a lonely man (rationalizing loneliness by constant protestations of misanthropy and concentration on his all-important work), brought up effectively as an only child as his brother Mycroft was

CLIVE BROOK AS SHERLOCK HOLMES *in a publicity still. The celebrated actor who played the detective on two occasions, in* The Return of Sherlock Holmes, *1929, and* Sherlock Holmes, *1932, was better known for other roles.*

seven years his senior and too old for true sibling companionship. His isolation from his parents is confirmed by the fact that, in all the thousands of words of Watson's reports, no mention is ever made of them. That his isolation is caused by the difficulties of his personality is affirmed by the reluctance of Stamford to encourage Watson to share lodgings with Holmes: "You mustn't blame me if you don't get on with him . . . You proposed this arrangement, so you must not hold me responsible." That Watson is nervous is also an undisputed fact: "It seems to me, Stamford . . . that you have some reason for washing your hands of this matter."

Having overcome all the normally insurmountable hurdles he encounters when formulating relationships, and settled down with Watson in what can only be described as a pseudo-marriage, it can readily be considered that this previously shunned and lonely person might very well have placed too high an emotional value on what the formidably heterosexual Watson naturally treated as a domestic arrangement of convenience. All the signs are there – showing off; playing hard to get; alternative moods of self-aggrandizement and feigned stupidity – to suggest that Holmes went through a courtship ritual with Watson, which went unnoticed by the simple focus of his attentions. Then comes the unexpected blow of the engagement. Watson, in Holmes's mind, is announcing that he is to divorce him, and marry, of all things, a woman.

The Adler case (*A Scandal in Bohemia*) could therefore not have come at a worse time from Holmes's psychological point of view. Perhaps on the way to recovery from being cut out of his friend's life and having his "marriage" destroyed by one woman, he is now bested and outwitted by another. This surely, if one is ever to espouse the Holmes-as-Ripper thesis, is the critical point, as it is easy to see how between March and August of 1888 Holmes's mind might further have deteriorated so that a few months later he was ready to start killing symbolic representations of the women who had disrupted both his personal and business life. That prostitutes should have been chosen is no surprise: they represented the antithesis of the purity of Mary Morstan;

the logical extension and the embodiment of Irene Adler's career as courtesan; and the dark side of the femininity in his own nature.

It is well known that in most instances of serial killing that remain unsolved, the murders come to a halt because the killer, coming to a realization of what he is doing, commits suicide. Indeed, this is the reason given in the Ripper case for strong suspicion against Montague Druitt. Holmes, as ever, must be considered too remarkable a man for such a simple resolution. The most likely theory is that he "caught himself", when investigating the case, and came to terms with what he had done. After a period of self-analysis, completed in 1891 by his faked disappearance from the world while he travelled, among other places, to Tibet, his rehabilitation was complete, and he then made amends by devoting the rest of his life to good.

Others have, of course, gone further. There is a theory that Holmes did not mend his ways, but stopped the serial killing because he feared capture. Then, having constructed the Reichenbach Falls mystery as an elaborate alibi, he slipped back into England to murder Mrs Watson, thereby regaining the affection of his lover, who rejoined him in Baker Street on his return. It is, indeed, strange that Holmes, freshly back from isolation in foreign parts, should appear to know so much about Mrs Watson's demise (see *The Empty House*, page 93). Others again have theorized that Professor Moriarty never existed, but was the black side of Holmes's own nature. The flight from Moriarty was Holmes's flight from his own black, murdering personality (the Ripper), and the struggle at the Falls was a Jungian symbol for Holmes's wrestling with all his darkest instincts in the wilderness. Having killed Moriarty (his desire to murder), he was free once more to re-enter society.

Whatever is believed about Holmes and the Ripper by others, the authors of this volume, though forced out of academic integrity to include these facts in order to present a well-rounded and comprehensive testament, nevertheless wish widely to distance themselves from such scurrilous speculation however well founded.

HOLMESIAN COLLECTABLES

Personal Collections and Investments

The enormous increase in the popularity of the Sherlock Holmes stories has been accompanied by a corresponding increase in the desire to collect any sort of items connected with Sherlock Holmes. These items vary greatly in quality and original price, but the limited quantities produced of some of the earlier items means that they are often now extremely valuable, and they have thus become investment items. Even some of the originally very cheap items are now greatly sought after by collectors. General production rates have recently become more attuned to the wider market for such items, but some pieces are still deliberately produced in limited numbers to increase their value after sale, and this is exactly what has happened. A general piece of advice is to buy everything of reasonable quality which one can afford, as it will

Sherlock Holmes:— "Judging by the line of evidence there's a Lady in that house!"

A UNIVERSAL FILM POSTER (*opposite*) *for one of the twelve Universal films that starred the Rathbone-Bruce partnership between 1942 and 1946.*

COMMEMORATIVE HOLMESIAN BADGES (*left*) *from around the world.*

EDWARDIAN COMIC POSTCARD (*far left*) *c.1910. Not one of Holmes's more famous cases.*

MINIATURE CHINA HEADS (*below*) *from left to right: Watson, Lestrade, Holmes, and Moriarty.*

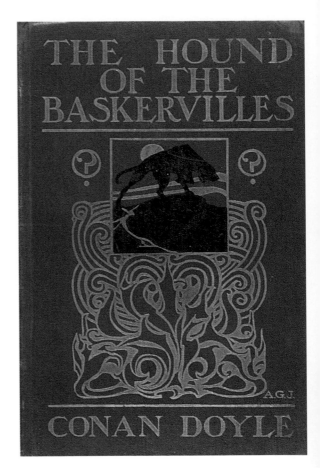

the subsequent owner. Dedications from one famous person to another, however, do increase the value of an item considerably. (It should be noted that all the prices given here are 1990 approximate values, with an exchange rate of two US dollars to the pound sterling.)

Manuscripts

Undoubtedly, the ultimate version of any of the stories in the Canon, in collectable terms, must be a Doylean manuscript. It should be noted here that the term "manuscript" means the original version of a story, whether that was handwritten or typewritten. The manuscript of *The Valley of Fear*, minus the epilogue, which appears to be lost for ever, was sold at auction in 1990 for over £150,000 ($300,000), including auction commission and tax! This exact manuscript was listed in *Scribner's Rare Book Catalogue* of 1943 at £550 ($1,100). Such items are rarely going to come onto the market, and their value is reasonably well known, so there is little chance of a bargain buy here. Although there is considerable interest amongst Holmesian scholars about the

A JAPANESE HOLMES *(above).*
Illustration by Kiyoshi Tanaka.

almost certainly increase its value within only a few years, and one may regret having to pay the higher price later or not even being able to obtain the item.

A further general point is concerned with the dedication of Holmesian items, such as the signing of books and programmes by authors, actors, and so on. If the item is intended for a personal collection, then a personalized dedication obviously makes the item of greater value to the person included in the dedication. If the item is for investment purposes, then it is usually better to have a more general dedication, which might more easily be applicable to

FIRST EDITION The Hound of the Baskervilles, *1902 (above right).*

manuscripts, only three stories have so far been published as facsimile versions. These are *The Adventure of the Priory School, The Adventure of the Lion's Mane,* and *The Adventure of the Dying Detective.* The first of these is already a rather expensive collector's item.

The Canon

The variety of single and collected editions of the stories in the Canon is enormous, and many readers are surprised to find that the texts vary between different editions. Some of these editions are more valuable because of these variations, and others are important as milestones in the publishing history of the Canon. It is possible to form an interesting private collection of editions without including the more exotic and extravagant rarities.

Probably the most desirable single edition for any collector to dream about is an original 1887 edition of *Beeton's Christmas Annual,* containing the first publication of a Sherlock Holmes story. This was published in paper covers, and a copy in good condition is extremely rare. A copy was sold at auction in 1990 for over £30,000 ($60,000), a notable increase on the original price of one shilling (10 cents), and a good investment increase on the 1943 catalogue listing of £87 (£175)!

The first editions of the long stories and of the collections of short stories are essential items in any serious Holmesian collector's library, but these too are becoming prohibitive in price. A copy of *The Hound of*

the *Baskervilles* (1902) in good condition would cost around £800 ($1,600), but an interesting collection can be made with some of the less rare editions, costing under £20 ($40) in many cases, and with some of the later, cheaper reproductions.

THE LAST ADVENTURE OF SHERLOCK HOLMES. *Illustrated cover for* Collier's.

Vol XXXIV No 18   JANUARY 28 1905   PRICE 10 CENTS

The Last Adventure of Sherlock Holmes

in this number

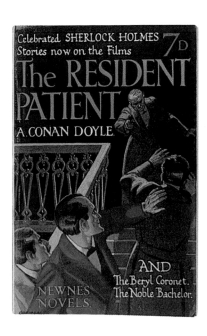
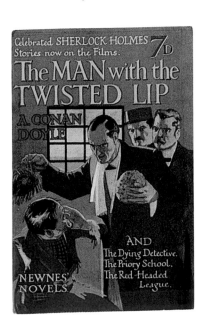
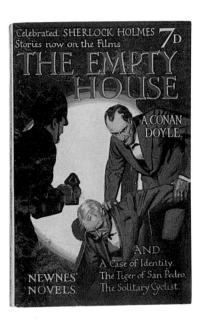

THE FIRST MOVIE TIE-INS *(left). Covers from the paperbacks for* The Resident Patient, The Man with the Twisted Lip, *and* The Empty House, *each starring Eille Norwood, 1921. Newnes published the tie-ins on the suggestion of Conan Doyle, but they were not a success.*

Pastiches, Parodies and Adaptations

A large number of Sherlock Holmes pastiches and parodies have been produced, most of them being of a very low standard, but some have become collector's items in their own right. A very popular series has been the *Solar Pons* stories by August Derleth, the original editions of which now fetch over £20 ($40) a copy, although newer paperback versions are now available. Others, such as Nicholas Meyer's *Seven-Per-Cent Solution*, are similarly more valuable in their first editions. Adaptations of the Canon, particularly in the form of scripts for television or radio, are extremely popular, with some author-signed adaptations being sold at over £100 ($200).

Magazines

Copies of the stories in the original *Strand Magazine* editions can be obtained for around £20–£50 ($40–$100), depending largely on condition, and everyone should perhaps attempt to find at least one of these to see how most of the stories were first seen. Complete sets are very rare items, and even a run of the nine *Strand*s containing *The Hound of the Baskervilles* can cost over £1,000 ($2,000). A less expensive way to obtain *Strand*s is in the six-monthly combined editions issued by the publishers in hardback covers, wherein one can often obtain six Sherlock Holmes short stories for around £30 ($60). The American equivalent of *The Strand Magazine* is *Collier's*, but copies of this magazine are often more difficult to find, even in America, and consequently more expensive.

Articles about Sherlock Holmes and Doyle are worth collecting from more general magazines, especially as their value is not often appreciated by those selling the

THE SIGN OF FOUR IN COMIC STRIP (far right) in issue 21, July 1944, from the American Classic Comics. *The edition also contains two non-Canonical stories.*

THE HOUND OF THE BASKERVILLES (below right) appeared in Classics Illustrated *issue 53, January 1947. The cover of the Greek edition (below far right) contains an interesting error: the missing red word, RACHE, is actually from* A Study in Scarlet.

THE NON-CANONICAL SHERLOCK STALKS THE JOKER (right) in The Joker Comic *number 6, April 1976. Holmes of the late twentieth century.*

magazines, but it can be hard work finding such items. In saving articles from current magazines, one should always save the whole magazine, rather than tear out the article, as complete magazines are not only more valuable but more interesting in placing the article in a historical context for later readers and collectors.

Another field for Holmesian interest is that of cartoon versions of the stories. There have been numerous issues of such items, but the value of these has risen very quickly, in line with the general increase in interest in the comic market. In 1990, some five-year-old £1 ($2) comics containing Sherlock Holmes were selling at around £20 ($40).

Film and Theatre Posters and Programmes

Some of the classic posters, such as an original Rathbone *The Hound of the Baskervilles*, now cost around £100 ($200), but there are reproductions available at £20 ($40), and some less expensive items can be obtained through film dealers, rather than

LOBBY CARD (*left*) *for the 1974 stage revival of* Sherlock Holmes. *An RSC production that first appeared at the Aldwych Theatre in London.*

CAMPAIGN BOOK (*above*). *The 1939 film was released as* The Adventures of Sherlock Holmes *in the U.S. and* Sherlock Holmes *in the U.K. A campaign book is supplied to the cinemas by the studios providing details of the story, the making of the film, publicity, and biographies of the actors.*

SPIDER WOMAN (*left*), 1944, *starring Basil Rathbone as Holmes and Gale Sondergaard as the eponymous villainess.*

SPANISH PROMOTIONAL LEAFLET *for* Sherlock Holmes Faces Death, *1943.*

POSTER FOR 1903 TOUR OF *SHERLOCK HOLMES (far right) starring Julian Royce, who toured with one of the Charles Frohman companies from 1902 to 1904. Mr Royce's was not one of the more renowned performances of Holmes.*

BELGIAN FILM POSTER *(right) for the 1959 film of* The Hound of the Baskervilles.

Holmesian dealers. Foreign language versions of film posters can certainly make a collection more interesting. Programmes for some of the newer, major productions are now produced on a large scale, and these can often be obtained for less than £1 ($2), but some of the older programmes are very valuable. It is worth obtaining local

56

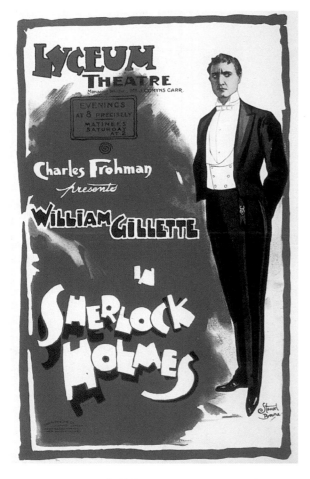

BY A. CONAN DOYLE
AND WILLIAM GILLETTE
ENTITLED

SHERLOCK HOLMES

BEING A HITHERTO UNPUBLISHED EPISODE
IN THE CAREER OF THE GREAT DETECTIVE
AND SHOWING HIS CONNECTION WITH THE

STRANGE CASE OF MISS FAULKNER

CHARACTERS IN THE PLAY				COMPANY APPEARING IN THE CAST
SHERLOCK HOLMES			...	WILLIAM GILLETTE
DOCTOR WATSON	...		...	KENNETH RIVINGTON
JOHN FORMAN	...		...	EUGENE MAYEUR
SIR EDWARD LEIGHTON	...			REGINALD DANCE
COUNT VON STAHLBURG	...		...	FREDERICK MORRIS
PROFESSOR MORIARTY	...		...	GEORGE SUMNER
JAMES LARRABEE	...		...	FRANCIS CARLYLE
SIDNEY PRINCE	..		...	QUINTON McPHERSON
ALFRED BASSICK	...		...	WILLIAM H. DAY
JIM CRAIGIN	...		...	CHRIS WALKER
THOMAS LEARY	...		...	HENRY WALTERS
"LIGHTFOOT" McTAGUE	...			WALTER DISON
JOHN	...		...	THOMAS QUINTON
PARSONS	...		...	G. MERTON
BILLY			...	CHARLES CHAPLIN
ALICE FAULKNER	...		...	MARIE DORO
MRS. FAULKNER	...		...	DE OLIA WEBSTER
MADGE LARRABEE	...			ADELAIDE PRINCE
THERESE	...		...	SYBIL CAMPBELL
MRS. SMEEDLEY	...		...	ETHEL LORRIMORE

THE PLACE IS LONDON
THE TIME TEN YEARS AGO

FIRST ACT—DRAWING ROOM AT THE LARRABEES'– EVENING

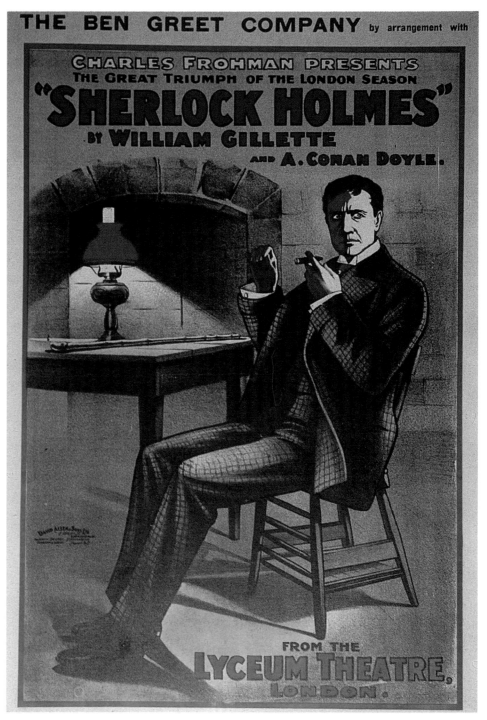

Photographs

production programmes, if only for the possibility that someone in the cast may later become more famous. (It is doubtful that anyone, apart from the lad's mother, originally bought a programme for the William Gillette play *Sherlock Holmes* because of the name of the young boy playing Wiggins, but Charles Chaplin's name certainly makes that a very collectable item today!) Again, with new productions, the value of a poster or programme can be increased by the autographs of the author or cast.

All pictures connected with Holmes are liable to become valuable, especially if they are signed. Even photographs of current Holmesian actors are selling for up to ten times their original price if they are signed, and loose photographs of some of the older stars are often very difficult to obtain. The market for such items has recently been more fully appreciated, with reproductions of many of the Rathbone publicity stills now becoming available at around £5 ($10).

BEN GREET COMPANY POSTER *1902.*

SHERLOCK HOLMES (above left). Poster for the first London production, 1901.

SHERLOCK HOLMES PROGRAMME *(above). An early revival of Gillette's play, this production is most notable for the fourteen-year-old actor who played Billy – Charles Chaplin.*

Games and Toys

SHERLOCK HOLMES
CONSULTING DETECTIVE. *Like
the Conan Doyles stories, the
American game has been
translated into many
languages such as Italian
(right) and German (far
right), which actually reads
"Sherlock Holmes, Criminal
Cabinet".*

There are usually several Holmesian games commercially available at any particular time, and these can quickly become collector's items once they go out of production,

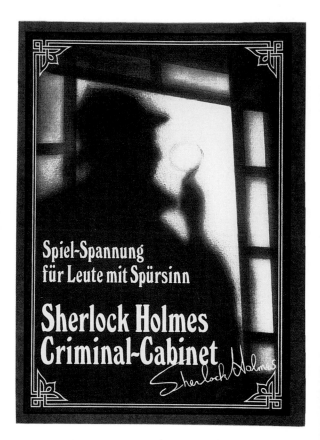

DONEGALL CHRISTMAS CARDS
*(right). Part of a series
designed by the American Dr
Julian Woolf for the eminent
Holmesian scholar Lord
Donegall.*

CARD GAME SET *(below),*
1904.

BOARD GAME *(far left)*, 1969.

BAKER STREET HOTEL MUG

HOLMES EARTHENWARE BUST, *(near left)* 1986.

thereby increasing their value. Early versions of such games are now very much sought after. The value of games often depends on whether there are any original parts missing, such as various paper forms which may have been filled in when the game was played. Toys vary greatly in value according to their condition, but not many particularly good Holmesian toys have been produced, and any older toys thus have a good rarity value.

MORIARTY, WATSON & HOLMES *(from left to right). Popular wall sculptures made by Bossons of Congleton.*

Ceramics and Models

Numerous mugs and plates have been issued to commemorate various anniversaries connected with Holmes and Doyle, and most of these have increased their value very rapidly. This is especially true of the limited editions, with some of the 1987 Centenary mugs, originally priced at around £10 ($20), selling in 1990 for more than double that price. Models of Holmes, Watson and Moriarty have always been popular, but the quality of production has varied a great deal. Production numbers have tended to be low, and so current prices are correspondingly high.

THE SCOTTISH HOLMES *(far left).*

THE JAPANESE HOLMES *(left). The inspiration for this red-headed statuette of Holmes, made in Japan, is unknown.*

PORTRAYALS OF HOLMES *The limited edition plate (far left) features some of the actors who have played the master sleuth. Key: 1. Basil Rathbone; 2. John Barrymore; 3. Arthur Wontner; 4. Eille Norwood; 5. Kenneth MacMillan; 6. John Wood; 7. John Neville; 8. Alan Wheatley; 9. Robert Stephens; 10. Clive Brook; 11. H. Hamilton Stewart; 12. Geoffrey Edwards; 13. H.A. Saintsbury; 14. William Gillette; 15. Carleton Hobbs; 16. Peter Cushing; 17. Christopher Plummer; 18. Douglas Wilmer; 19. Jeremy Brett; 20. Nigel Bruce (Dr Watson).*

HOLMES IN BRONZE *from the Sherlock Holmes Museum in London. The bust was made by the British sculptor Martin Lorenz.*

HOLMESIAN TEAPOT (*near right*). *A fine example of Sherlockian kitsch from the Far East.*

HOLMES DUTCH DOLL (*right*). *Early twentieth-century hand-made Dutch doll loosely based on the Paget illustrations.*

SHERLOCK HOLMES PUZZLE, (*far right*), *Early cigarette card from Gallaher's.*

WALL RELIEF (*near right*). *The sculpture is made entirely of different metals.*

BLUE MUG (*right*) *was from the former Moriarty's Baker Street Tube Station Pub in London.*

VARSITY POSTER (*right*). *Holmes quickly became a vehicle for advertising as this 1907 cigarette poster illustrates.*

JOHN PLAYER & SONS CIGARETTE CARD (*far right*). *No.21 of a series of 25 cards entitled "Characters from Fiction", this illustration is based on an original one by H.M. Brock.*

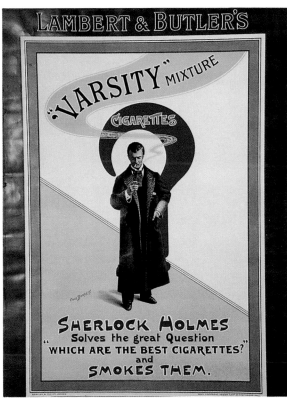

Advertisements

Holmes has always been a popular figure in advertisements, and some of these can be obtained literally for nothing, although dealers do charge considerable sums for some of them. Again, it is worthwhile keeping the whole magazine if it contains a Holmesian advertisement. A specialist form of advertising was the cigarette card, and

Holmes appears in some of these. The Alexander Boguslavsky set of 25 Doylean characters will cost at least £50 ($100) for the green-backed set, and £70 ($140) for the scarcer black-backed version, and dealers in such cards are all well aware of the values. Holmes has also appeared on beer mats, and there are specialist dealers for these, with prices being around £1 ($2) for each mat (preferably without any alcoholic content!).

GOVERNMENT WEALTH WARNING
Collecting Holmesiana
Can Severely Damage
Your Bank Balance

CHESTERFIELD HOLMES (*left*). *Basil Rathbone advertising the cigarettes.*

"THE ORIGINAL SHERLOCK HOLMES" PIPE (*below*). *An elementary advertisement for Peterson of Dublin.*

Collier's

Household Number for November

Sherlock Holmes

In this Number Solves
The Mystery of

The

Norwood Builder

THE CANON
Summaries of The Stories

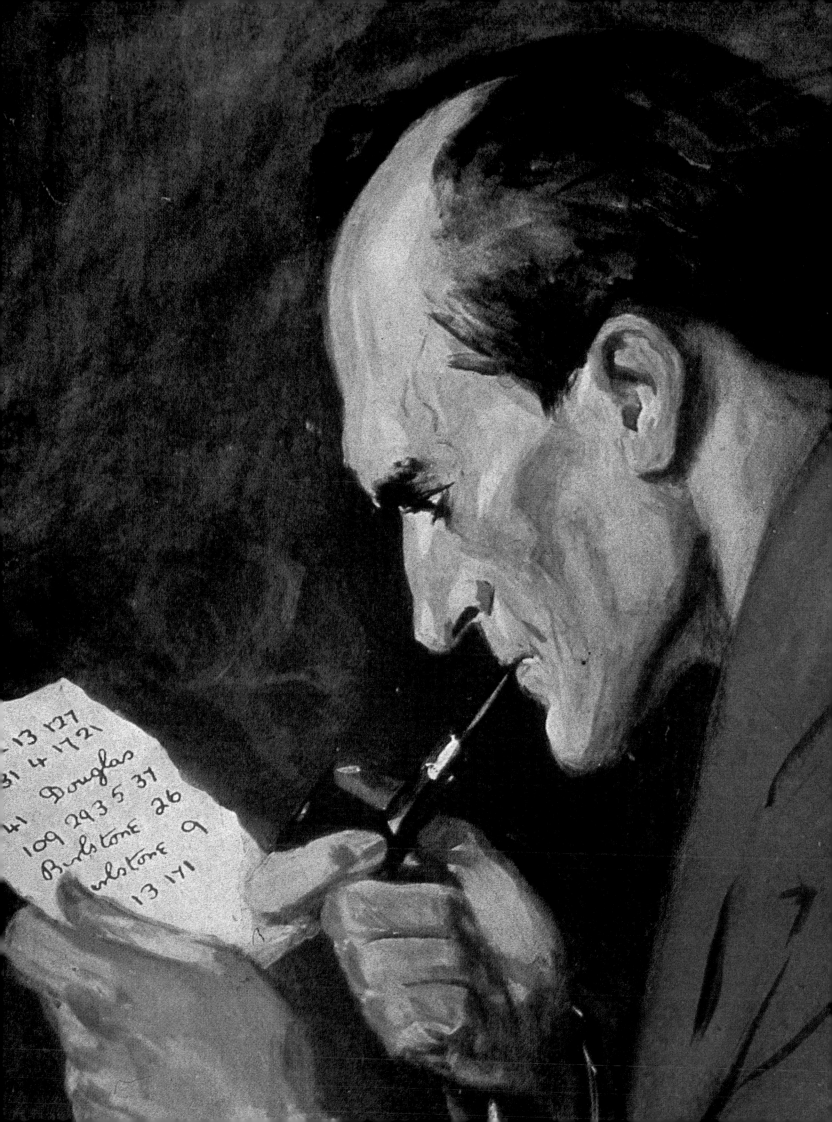

AN INTRODUCTION TO THE CASE SUMMARIES

These summaries are in no way intended to provide alternatives to reading the cases themselves, for nothing could compete with the pleasures given by the original cases. It is also most strongly recommended that none of these summaries should be read before the original case, for that could easily spoil much of the enjoyment.

The main purpose of the summaries is to provide a version of how each case might be seen, in order to have something with which to compare and contrast one's own interpretation. Part of the greatness of the cases is that they seem to be capable of supplying something to many different types of readers, and it is hoped that these summaries will help each reader to identify something of that for themselves.

Included with each summary are some narrative points of particular interest in each case, as well as an indication of the publishing history of the story. There is also a listing of the major characters in each case, as it can often be difficult to recall some of these. All of the character names are not given, as there are over 400 of them

in the Canon! Holmes and Watson are not mentioned in the lists of characters, and very often Watson's name is omitted from parts of the summary, where it is obvious or unimportant to the facts of the case that he was present.

The cases are listed here in the chronological order in which they were first published.

HOLMES AS ILLUSTRATED BY FRANK WILES *(opposite). The frontispiece to the first instalment of* The Valley of Fear. *It was the only illustration in colour to accompany a Sherlock Holmes story in* The Strand Magazine.

A REVERIE *(left). Illustrating some of the earlier cases that appeared in* The Strand Magazine.

CIGARETTE CARDS *(far left): Man with the Twisted Lip, King of Bohemia, and Mary Morstan.*

THE STRAND MAGAZINE *(below), September 1914, cover containing the first instalment of* The Valley of Fear.

THE SIGN OF FOUR

First published: *Lippincott's Monthly Magazine* in February 1890
under the title *The Sign of the Four*
Main Characters: Mary Morstan, Captain Morstan, Major Sholto, Thaddeus Sholto,
Bartholomew Sholto, Jonathan Small, Inspector Athelney Jones, Tonga

The narrative begins with Holmes taking cocaine to relieve the boredom of inactivity, but he soon becomes totally engrossed when Miss Mary Morstan arrives at 221B to inform him about her situation. Her father, Captain Morstan, had disappeared ten years previously on returning to London from duty in India. For each of the last six years she had received a large pearl by post, and she had now been asked to meet her benefactor. Holmes discovers that Captain Morstan's only friend in London, Major Sholto, had mysteriously died a few days before the first pearl had been sent and that Morstan had had some connection with a group of men known as "The Four".

Holmes and Watson accompany Mary to her rendezvous, where one of the twin sons of Major Sholto, Thaddeus, explains that his father had illegally obtained possession of the Agra treasure, with Morstan's assistance, whilst they were commanding a penal colony in the Andaman Islands. When Morstan returned to England he had died from a weak heart whilst arguing over his share of the treasure, and Sholto had secretly disposed of the body. On his deathbed, Sholto had asked his sons to ensure that Mary got her share of the treasure, but then died of shock on seeing a wooden-legged man at his window, before he could reveal the treasure's hiding place. A note reading "The sign of the four" was later found on his body. Thaddeus had been sending Mary the pearls from the only piece of the treasure that was not hidden, but his brother, Bartholomew, had apparently just discovered the rest of the treasure.

THE SLEUTH (*above*). *One of Royal Doulton's best selling toby jugs.*

SOMETHING'S AMISS. *Eille Norwood in* The Sign of Four, *1923. Humberston Wright plays the corpse.*

STOLL PICTURE PRODUCTION

THE SIGN OF FOUR
ADAPTED FROM SIR ARTHUR CONAN DOYLE'S IMMORTAL STORY

Holmes, Watson, Mary and Thaddeus travel to Bartholomew's house, where they find him dead, with a poisoned thorn in his neck and a note reading "The sign of the four". The treasure is also gone. Holmes finds the marks of a one-legged man and what appears to be a bare-footed child. He deduces that the man is Jonathan Small, since that was the name of the only English-man included in a listing of "The Four" found in Morstan's papers. Holmes follows their trail and finds that they have boarded a launch called the *Aurora*.

In the meantime, Inspector Athelney Jones arrests Thaddeus and detains most of Bartholomew's household in connection with the murder. Holmes sends out his band of street urchins, the Baker Street Irregulars, to search for the *Aurora*. He discovers that amongst the Andaman Islanders there are some very short savages who use poisoned darts to kill their victims, and concludes that the footprints of the "child" must have been those of such an Andaman savage. Watson keeps Mary informed of proceedings and records an increasing affection for her, but remains constrained by the thought of her potential inheritance.

Holmes eventually locates the *Aurora*, and when Small sails he is chased by Holmes, Watson and Jones in a police launch. When the savage attempts to use his blow-pipe, he

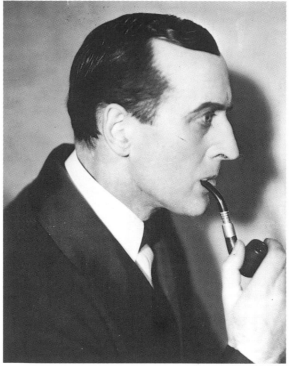

THE INTENSITY OF HOLMES. *Arthur Wontner in the 1932 film* The Sign of Four. *Wonter was one of the more successful actors to portray Holmes, closely resembling a Paget illustration despite the ill-fitting toupee.*

is shot, and Small is then caught. Watson takes the treasure box to Mary, but they discover that Small has emptied the contents into the Thames. As Mary is no longer to be rich, Watson admits that he loves her, and she reciprocates. The case ends with Watson announcing that he is about to be married, Jones getting the credit for arresting Small, and Holmes returning to his cocaine-bottle.

This case has the most notorious example of Holmes's drug abuse, but, as has been explained elsewhere, this habit declined when he became more famous and had better things to occupy him. It provides some excellent examples of his deductive abilities, including the incident where we find that Watson once had an older brother. There are also many indications of Holmes's sense of humour, and of his delight in being involved with something challenging. There is a great deal of information provided about Watson, and especially about his romantic inclinations. Watson's feelings for Mary are extremely well recorded, as are Holmes's lack of enthusiasm for the loss of a colleague in this manner. There are numerous problems in the case, such as the nature of the savage Tonga's poison, which seems to have almost magical powers, but which does not appear to exist in any recorded poison.

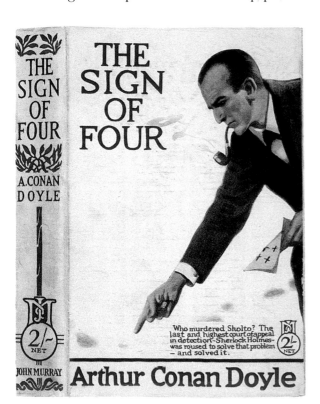

THE SIGN OF FOUR
THE SIGN OF FOUR
A. CONAN DOYLE
Who murdered Sholto? The last and highest court of appeal in detection–Sherlock Holmes–was roused to solve that problem – and solved it.
JOHN MURRAY
Arthur Conan Doyle

DUST COVER *for the John Murray "two-shilling novels" edition of 1924.*

A SCANDAL IN BOHEMIA

First published: *The Strand Magazine* in July 1891
Main Characters: Irene Adler, the King of Bohemia

The King of Bohemia engages Holmes to retrieve a mildly compromising photograph from the King's former mistress, Irene Adler, since any scandal might jeopardize the King's forthcoming marriage. Holmes follows Irene and becomes involved as a witness at her marriage to Godfrey Norton. He later gains entry to her house, disguised as an elderly clergyman who is injured whilst attempting to rescue Irene from ruffians hired by himself. He tricks Irene into revealing the location of the photograph when Watson starts a fire scare from outside the house. When Holmes returns to Irene's house with the King the next day, however, he finds that she has discovered his ruse and already left for the Continent with her husband. She has left a note for Holmes, explaining that she would never use the photograph, unless threatened by the King, and she has also left another photograph of herself in the hiding place. Holmes claimed this photograph as part of his reward from the King, and thereafter always referred to Irene as "The Woman".

This case has generated numerous theories about Holmes's attitude towards women. The respect which he demonstrates for Irene who, to some extent, bettered him, contrasts markedly with his more often expressed suspicion and dislike for women in general. Watson records that this was just an intellectual admiration, but the keeping of the photograph implies more, although any emotions were certainly kept well suppressed. Holmes also shows that he was no respecter of mere rank, since he is quite openly rude to the King at times. The case shows something of Holmes's sense of humour, including an outburst of laughter which contrasts with the saturnine appearance more often described by Watson.

"THEN HE STOOD BEFORE THE FIRE." *Holmes assessing a heavier and married Watson. Illustrated by Sidney Paget.*

THE WOMAN (*far right*). "*When he speaks of Irene Adler, or when he refers to her photograph, it is always under the honourable title of* the woman."

THE RED-HEADED LEAGUE

First published: *The Strand Magazine* in August 1891
Main Characters: Jabez Wilson, Vincent Spaulding, John Clay, Peter Jones

The red-headed Jabez Wilson informs Holmes that he has been employed for some eight weeks, part-time, in copying out the *Encyclopaedia Britannica*. His employer has been The Red-Headed League, a philanthropic organization for men with red hair, which paid him well but insisted upon him working alone in an office from 10AM until 2PM each day. He had been informed about this job by his assistant, Vincent Spaulding, who ran Wilson's pawnbroking business whilst the latter was working at the League's office. Wilson had arrived at the office that morning to find a notice declaring the League dissolved.

Holmes asks for further details about Spaulding, then visits the area of Wilson's shop and confirms Spaulding's true identity as that of a notorious criminal called John Clay. Holmes persuades Peter Jones, a police agent, and the local bank manager to hide themselves with Holmes and Watson in the vaults of the bank behind Wilson's shop, where there are large, temporary deposits of gold coins. Clay and his accomplice complete a tunnel into the vault and are arrested. Holmes had deduced that Clay was decoying Wilson away from the shop, and confirmed that he was tunnelling by the marks on the knees of Clay's trousers. He found that the direction of the tunnel was to the rear of the shop by the absence of any hollow sound when he tapped the pavement in front of the shop with his stick.

This case provides some excellent examples of Holmes's deductive abilities, especially with the classical introductory analysis of Wilson's background, very much in the style of Dr Bell, the tutor of Watson's Literary Agent, Dr Doyle. The suggestion can be made that Peter Jones is a Watsonian mistake for Athelney Jones, especially as the Sholto case is specifically mentioned. There is also a question of the meaning of Clay shouting to his accomplice that he will "swing for it", as the crime they are committing is certainly not a capital one. He may

have been acknowledging the fact that one of his earlier crimes was punishable by hanging, or, possibly, that he may have already murdered Wilson to facilitate the final phase of the robbery.

"MR. MERRYWEATHER STOPPED TO LIGHT A LANTERN." *The bank director accompanies Holmes, Watson and Jones as they wait for the robbers.*

"HE CURLED HIMSELF UP IN HIS CHAIR." *To contemplate the case (below) as does Jeremy Brett for the Granada Television series (below left).*

THE FIVE ORANGE PIPS

First published: *The Strand Magazine* in November 1891
Main Characters: John Openshaw, Joseph Openshaw, Elias Openshaw,
Captain James Calhoun

John Openshaw arrives at 221B late on a stormy night. He relates that his father, Joseph, has retired comfortably, and that his uncle, Elias, had made a considerable fortune in America before returning to live in Sussex because of his objections to negro emancipation in America. Some four years previously, Elias had received an envelope from India, marked with "KKK" and containing five orange pips. He had imme-

"HIS EYES BENT UPON THE GLOW OF THE FIRE." *Holmes contemplates the mystery of the ominous fruit seeds.*

diately burned some papers from a locked box, then made out a will leaving everything to Joseph. Shortly afterwards he was found dead in a shallow pond. Some years after this, John's father had received a similar envelope from Dublin with an additional note saying "Put the papers on the sun dial". Subsequently, he had been found dying of a shattered skull after a fall into a chalk-pit. John had now received a similar demand from London.

Holmes discovers that "KKK" stands for the Ku Klux Klan, an American racist organization which warns men that it has condemned with orange pips. He also notes that all the demands came from seaports, and that a major disruption of the KKK in America had coincided with Elias's return to England. That night, John's body is recovered from the Thames. Holmes ascertains that the murderer was Captain James Calhoun of the *Lone Star*, because the posting dates of the letters coincided with visits of his ship to the particular ports. Holmes sends five orange pips to Calhoun, but the *Lone Star* is lost at sea on its next voyage.

This case is one of Holmes's failures, in that he loses his client before he concludes the case, but this also makes the Canon more realistic, in that no-one could meet with success in all of the numerous cases which Holmes investigates. Watson's own susceptibility to human weakness is also indicated here, with his condemnation of Holmes as a "self-poisoner" by tobacco, even though he himself admits to smoking strong tobacco before joining Holmes at 221B.

THE MAN WITH THE TWISTED LIP

First published: *The Strand Magazine* in December 1891
Main Characters: Neville St Clair, Mrs St Clair, Hugh Boone, Inspector Bradstreet

At the request of his wife's friend, Mrs Whitney, Watson recovers her husband from an opium den, and there finds Holmes, in disguise, searching for a missing Neville St Clair. After despatching Whitney home, Holmes and Watson travel to St Clair's house to question his wife. St Clair journeyed to London supposedly on business each day, but whilst visiting a riverside London location Mrs St Clair was surprised to see her husband at a window above the opium den. After the police had been called, the room was searched. The only man in the room was a beggar called Hugh Boone, who had a badly disfigured face. Blood stains were found, and St Clair's jacket which had been recovered from the river weighed down with numerous coins.

Holmes informs Mrs St Clair that he believes her husband to be dead, but finds that she has just received a reassuring note and his signet ring. The next morning Holmes drives to Bow Street police station where Boone is being kept, and, accompanied by Inspector Bradstreet, he scrubs Boone's face to reveal that he is actually St Clair, who had been earning a comfortable living through begging. St Clair promises never to use the disguise again.

"THE PIPE WAS STILL BETWEEN HIS LIPS." *Watson awakes to find that Holmes has been up all night smoking shag and analyzing the clues.*

This is another of the cases in which there is no real crime committed. It is also the case in which Mrs Watson calls her husband James, to the lasting delight of Watsonian theorists everywhere. Grave doubts have been caused over Watson's suggestion that Boone's make-up be removed with a sponge and cold water; since Holmes was such an expert with make-up he would surely have gone to the police station with an appropriate removal cream.

THE ADVENTURE OF THE BLUE CARBUNCLE

First published: *The Strand Magazine* in January 1892
Main Characters: Peterson, Henry Baker, John Horner, James Ryder

Whilst returning home from a Christmas celebration, Peterson, the commissionaire, witnesses a man attacked by roughs. The man drops his hat and the goose he is carrying whilst trying to defend himself, and then accidentally breaks a window with his stick at which point Peterson intervenes – causing the roughs as well as the startled man to flee. Holmes advises Peterson to eat the goose, then he analyses the hat, which he discovers belongs to Henry Baker.

Peterson later discovers the Blue Carbuncle, a huge gem stolen from the Duchess of Morcar, in the goose and brings it to Holmes, who recognizes it. John Horner, a plumber who was working in the hotel room from which the stone was stolen, has been arrested on the evidence of James

"SEE WHAT MY WIFE FOUND IN ITS CROP!" The commissionaire hands over the precious stone after his wife found something hard in the bird's gullet (above).

" 'HAVE MERCY!' HE SHRIEKED." Ryder importunes Holmes for leniency (above right).

"HE BURST INTO CONVULSIVE SOBBING." And Holmes lets him leave (right). A moment of sympathy from the consulting detective?

Ryder, the hotel attendant. Holmes advertises for the owner of the hat and, when finding him innocent, replaces his lost bird with another. Holmes then traces the supplier of the original bird, where he finds James Ryder also looking for the supplier. On being confronted, Ryder admits to stealing the stone and stuffing it into a goose as a hiding place, after which he had taken the wrong goose. Holmes lets Ryder off with a severe cautioning and the stone is returned to its owner, with Peterson getting the offered reward and Horner being released.

This case involves an extended and brilliant example of Holmes's deductive powers in his analysis of Baker's hat. This story is also another example of Holmes acting as his own court of law, in deciding Ryder's fate.

It can be suggested that here Holmes readily accepts a form of redistributing wealth, in that he states that the Duchess can easily afford the large reward given to Peterson.

THE ADVENTURE OF THE SPECKLED BAND

First published: *The Strand Magazine* in February 1892
Main Characters: Helen Stoner, Julia Stoner, Grimesby Roylott

Miss Helen Stoner informs Holmes that her late mother had bequeathed a large income to herself, her twin sister, and her step-father, Dr Grimesby Roylott, with whom Helen and her sister had continued to live after their mother's death. Julia had become engaged two years previously, and had informed Helen that she had heard a mysterious whistling sound at night. Shortly afterwards Julia died, muttering "the speckled band". Helen had recently become betrothed, and had been moved by her stepfather into Julia's old room, where she too had heard a whistling sound.

After Helen's departure from 221B, Roylott arrives to warn Holmes to stay out of his affairs, but Holmes and Watson later travel to Roylott's house to examine the fatal bedroom. That night they secretly occupy the room and find a snake crawling down a false bell-rope towards the bed. Holmes drives the snake back into the adjoining room, where it kills Roylott, who had trained it to seek out victims and then be recalled by a whistle. He had tried to kill the sisters to prevent them marrying and taking away their inheritance.

This case is the one which has most frequently been voted the best of the short Holmesian stories. It certainly has every element of drama and suspense, but it also has one of the most contorted methods of murdering someone ever invented. It shows Holmes's disregard for the opinions of others: when Roylott bends a poker to show his strength, Holmes does not bend it straight in front of Roylott, but waits until he has gone. His verbal responses to Roylott's threatening bluster certainly demonstrate a superb coolness. There are some difficulties however with the creatures in this case since there is no such snake as a swamp adder.

THE ADVENTURE OF THE ENGINEER'S THUMB

First published: *The Strand Magazine* in March 1892
Main Characters: Victor Hatherley, Colonel Lysander Stark, Mr Ferguson/
Dr Becher, Elise, Inspector Bradstreet

Victor Hatherley, a hydraulic engineer, is brought to Watson's surgery having lost a thumb in a murderous attack. Watson takes Hatherley to Holmes, where the engineer states that he had been asked by Colonel Stark to investigate a faulty hydraulic press at his house. Hatherley was taken to the house by a long route from Reading railway station, in the dark, and was introduced to Stark's manager, Mr Ferguson. He was secretly warned to leave the house by a lady called Elise. Hatherley soon discovered the fault, but also found that the machine was being used to press counterfeit coins, and was thereupon locked inside the press with the ram ready to crush him. The lady freed him, but while hanging from a window ledge he was attacked by Stark who severed Hatherley's thumb with a cleaver.

Holmes recalls that another hydraulic engineer had disappeared mysteriously a year ago. On reaching Reading with Hatherley and Inspector Bradstreet, Holmes deduces that the house is close to the station, and that Hatherley had been driven in circles on his previous visit. There they discover the charred remains of the house. They also find that the householder, Mr Ferguson, who is known locally as Dr Becher, has fled with the rest of the gang, and they are never heard of again.

This is an extremely unsatisfactory case, in that the criminals appear to suffer only the inconvenience of having to move their location. There is the common problem in this case of a police officer apparently accompanying Holmes outside of the officer's district, but this time it could be suggested that the plain clothes officer who accompanies them might have been previously called to London from the Reading area. There are differences in the text between *The Strand Magazine* and the book version, in connection with the position of Hatherley's hands on the windowsill, which can be used to explain how Stark actually managed to reach Hatherley's thumb whilst he was hanging there. The Paget drawing, however, also shows how it could have been done.

THE ADVENTURE OF THE NOBLE BACHELOR

First published: *The Strand Magazine* in April 1892
Main Characters: Lord Robert St Simon, Hatty Doran, Flora Miller, Frank Moulton, Inspector Lestrade

CONAN DOYLE CHARACTERS

LESTRADE

After the wedding of Lord Robert St Simon and Hatty Doran, the daughter of an American millionaire, the bride had disappeared. Flora Miller, who had tried earlier to force her way into the reception, had been arrested by Lestrade. St Simon calls on Holmes and admits that he had been very friendly with Flora, and recalls that at the wedding Hatty had been handed flowers by an unknown man, but had dropped them. Holmes states that he has solved the case but does not yet know the location of the missing bride.

Hatty's dress is then found in the Serpentine, with a note written on the back of a hotel bill arranging a rendezvous. Holmes invites St Simon to supper, where they are joined by Hatty and Frank Moulton, her husband by an earlier marriage who had been thought dead. Holmes had traced him by checking the hotels which charged the high prices shown on the bill. St Simon departs, feeling insulted.

This is yet another case in which no intentional crime is committed, and we have another example of Holmes's dislike for snobbery. Here, as in other cases, there are also, quite correctly, objections to the way in which Holmes addresses nobility. St Simon is referred to as "Lord St Simon", whereas, as the second son of a duke (the Duke of Balmoral), he should actually be referred to as Lord Robert St Simon or simply as Lord Robert. Similarly, it should be Lady Robert, not Lady St Simon.

THE ADVENTURE OF THE BERYL CORONET

First published: *The Strand Magazine* in May 1892
Main Characters: Alexander Holder, Arthur Holder, Sir George Burnwell, Mary

Alexander Holder, a banker, arrives at 221B to inform Holmes that he has loaned £50,000 to a client against the security of the famous Beryl Coronet. He had taken it home, where he lived with his son, Arthur, and his niece, Mary. Arthur, under the bad influence of a Sir George Burnwell, had previously asked for money to pay off gambling debts, and had been refused. Awakened in the early hours, Holder had found Arthur holding the coronet, from which three stones were missing, and so Arthur had been arrested.

Holmes examines the house and deduces that the coronet must have been broken outside the house. The next day, Mary disappears. Holmes asks for £4,000 and produces the missing gems. From footprints in the garden, Holmes deduced that Mary had met Sir George and given him the coronet, but Arthur had retrieved it, unknowingly having snapped off the three stones in the struggle. Arthur had refused to inform on Mary and had gone to prison for her. Holmes retrieved the stones from a dealer at £1,000 each, and charged another £1,000 for his services.

With his often repeated claim that he does his job for its own sake, one must assume that Holmes's large fee in this case was a reasonable charge against a man who was foolish enough to place something so valuable in a weak bureau at home, rather than in the safe at the bank. Much consternation has been caused by the reference at the start of this case to a bow window at 221B, since there were no houses with bow windows in Baker Street. Bow-topped windows, however, were very popular at that time.

"SOMETHING LIKE FEAR SPRANG UP IN THE YOUNG LADY'S EYES." *Mary Holder begins to realize the deductive power of Holmes's mind (far left).*

"I CLAPPED A PISTOL TO HIS HEAD." *One of Holmes's not-so-subtle methods of acquiring information (left).*

THE ADVENTURE OF THE COPPER BEECHES

First published: *The Strand Magazine* in June 1892
Main Characters: Violet Hunter, Jephro Rucastle, Mrs Rucastle, Alice Rucastle, Mr Fowler, Carlo the mastiff

"TAKING UP A GLOWING CINDER WITH THE TONGS." *Holmes complains about Watson's sensationalisation of his racey recordings of the cases (below).*

Miss Violet Hunter asks for Holmes's advice over accepting an appointment as a governess at the Copper Beeches near Winchester. Her potential employer, Jephro Rucastle, was offering high wages but required her to cut off her long hair and to wear such dresses as he and his wife might decide. After initially refusing she had been offered an even higher wage by Rucastle. Holmes promises help if needed, and is later called to Winchester. Violet explains that the adult daughter of the house had apparently gone to America because of an aversion to Rucastle, her step-father. Violet had cut her hair and been made to sit in a window wearing a particular blue dress. When she found that a young man was observing her, she was told to signal him to go away. Later she discovered that someone was locked in hidden rooms.

Holmes concludes that Violet has been tricked into impersonating Rucastle's

79

THE ADVENTURE OF THE MUSGRAVE RITUAL

First published: *The Strand Magazine* in May 1893
Main Characters: Reginald Musgrave, Brunton, Rachel

Holmes recounts to Watson another early case, where his former college acquaintance, Reginald Musgrave, had reported problems with his butler, Brunton, a well-educated man who was over-fond of affairs with the female servants. Musgrave had dismissed Brunton after finding him looking through private family papers, including the seemingly meaningless Musgrave Ritual recited on inheriting the estate. Brunston had then disappeared, as had Rachel, a maid recently jilted by the butler. The lake had been dragged, but only a strange collection of objects had been found in a bag.

Holmes determines that the ritual contains directions, which he follows, to discover Brunton's body under a floor. Brunton had also followed the directions, found a treasure, then been trapped in the vault by Rachel, who had then thrown the treasure into the lake before fleeing. The treasure proved to include the corroded ancient crown of England, entrusted to the Musgraves by Charles I before he was executed.

This is another unusual case, in that Watson does not take part in the proceedings. Musgrave takes his place to some extent, but he is not an entirely suitable replacement, being aristocratically remote, and, like all the Musgraves, lacking the intelligence to realize the significance of the ritual as Brunton had done. The fact that such an aristocrat would automatically attend Oxford or Cambridge, albeit without any requirements for scholarly abilities at that time, is used to suggest that Holmes, who was a college acquaintance, must also have attended one of these two universities.

THE ADVENTURE OF THE REIGATE SQUIRES

First published: *The Strand Magazine* in June 1893. First published as *The Adventure of the Reigate Squire* in England, and as *The Reigate Puzzle* in USA
Main Characters: Colonel Hayter, William Kirwan, Mr Cunningham, Alec Cunningham

Watson invites Holmes to recover from overwork at the home of his friend, Colonel Hayter, near Reigate. There they hear of a burglary at the Actons' house in which some peculiar items are taken. The next day they

THE PIECE OF THE NOTE FOUND IN THE DEAD MAN'S HAND. *To solve this case Holmes applied his elementary graphological skills.*

hear that a coachman, William Kirwan, has been murdered during a burglary at the Cunninghams' house, the fleeing murderer having been seen by Mr Cunningham and his son, Alec. The corner of a note was found in Kirwan's hand, mentioning an appointment. Holmes writes out a reward note, which Mr Cunningham has to correct, then, whilst examining the house, Holmes disappears. Watson then hears Holmes cry for help and, along with the Colonel and the Inspector, rushes to the landing to find Holmes being attacked by the Cunninghams. On being rescued Holmes produces the letter from which a corner had been torn. He had noticed that the words on the torn corner had been written alternately by two people, and had assumed that the peculiar objects stolen from the Actons' house had been taken to detract attention from the real purpose of the burglary, which was to obtain an important document involved in a land dispute. Holmes had disappeared to search for the torn note in the Cunninghams' rooms, having become suspicious when he realized that they could not have seen a fleeing murderer from their rooms as they had claimed. Kirwan had been killed because he had followed his masters when they burgled the Actons' house and attempted to blackmail them.

Holmes is rather cruel to Watson in this case, when he upsets a bowl of fruit and blames Watson for it, in order to distract attention whilst he disappears. It also has the distinction of involving a colonel who is neither a villain nor extremely rude. The copies of the letter which appear in the published versions do not include all the graphological details described by Holmes, which suggests that the original must have been lost.

CONAN DOYLE CHARACTERS

DR. WATSON

THE ADVENTURE OF THE CROOKED MAN

First published: *The Strand Magazine* in July 1893
Main Characters: Colonel Barclay, Mrs Barclay, Miss Morrison, Henry Wood,
Teddy the mongoose

Holmes informs Watson that he is investigating the murder in Aldershot of Colonel Barclay, who had risen from the ranks to command the Mallows. Mrs Barclay had returned home and had a row with her husband. After hearing a scream, the servants found the living room door locked on the inside, and on entering through the French window, found the Colonel dead and Mrs Barclay unconscious. The key to the door could not be found, but a club was lying near the Colonel and Mrs Barclay is suspected of murder.

On examining the house next day, Holmes finds the prints of a man and a strange creature which had run up the curtains. He deduces that the Colonel had either been killed by this man, who must have taken the door key, or died from hitting his head after fainting from seeing this man. Mrs Barclay's friend, Miss Morrison, mentions that they had seen a badly deformed man the night before, who had been well known to Mrs Barclay. Holmes interviews this man, Henry Wood, who had been a corporal in India when Barclay had been a sergeant and a rival for the future Mrs Barclay's hand. During a siege, Wood had been sent for help by Barclay, then was betrayed by him. He had become a prisoner and was ill-treated until deformed, but had eventually escaped and returned to England. On meeting Mrs Barclay he had informed her of his fate and she had confronted the Colonel. When Wood arrived in the room the Colonel had died of shock. The strange animal was Wood's pet mongoose. Wood does not have to give evidence, as Mrs Barclay is cleared when the postmortem reveals that the Colonel died of apoplexy.

Some texts change the Mallows to the Munsters. The latter was a real regiment the history of which does not fit that of Colonel Barclay's regiment. Watson, as an old soldier, no doubt invented the former to protect the name of the actual regiment involved. The knowledge of the Bible exhibited by Holmes does not coincide with his normal attitude towards religion, but it may have been the dogmatic teaching of such biblical knowledge which originally drove him towards his rationalistic attitudes.

THE ADVENTURE OF THE RESIDENT PATIENT

First published: *The Strand Magazine* in August 1893
Main Characters: Dr Percy Trevelyan, Mr Blessington, Sutton, the Whittington bank gang

CONAN DOYLE CHARACTERS

PROFESSOR MORIARTY

Dr Percy Trevelyan informs Holmes that a wealthy patient, Mr Blessington, had established him in a good practice in Blessington's house, partly in exchange for the treatment of Blessington's heart condition. Blessington had recently become inexplicably agitated and increased the house security. Not long after, Trevelyan had been examining a visiting Russian nobleman who was accompanied by his son. The Russian had gone into a trance during the examination and Trevelyan left the room to obtain medicines. When he returned the Russians had gone. Blessington then found signs of intruders in his bedroom.

Holmes questions Blessington, but the latter is evasive. The next morning Blessington is found hanged in his bedroom, and Holmes deduces that the supposed Russians were responsible. Blessington, or

Sutton as his real name was, had been a member of the Whittington bank gang. Years earlier Blessington had informed on the gang and became anxious on reading of their recent release from prison. Meanwhile, the gang members escape London, but are then believed to be lost at sea.

This case temporarily contained the mind-reading episode from *The Cardboard Box*, but the seasons described in the initial paragraph became confused. This version can still be found in some texts. Holmes can be accused himself for unjustly accusing the page at Blessington's house before he knows that the page has run away, since it is seemingly only the flight which would suggest guilt. However, Holmes does not always give all the indications of guilt which he has seen.

THE ADVENTURE OF THE GREEK INTERPRETER

First published: *The Strand Magazine* in September 1893
Main Characters: Mycroft Holmes, Mr Melas, Harold Latimer, William Kemp, Paul Kratides, Sophy Kratides, Inspector Gregson

Watson is introduced for the first time to Holmes's brother, Mycroft. Mr Melas, Mycroft's neighbour, reports that he had recently been taken by Harold Latimer in a closed carriage to a country house to interpret for a Greek gentleman. He had found the gentleman guarded and gagged, able to communicate only in writing. He surreptitiously discovered that the man was Paul Kratides from Athens, and that he was being forcibly restrained. A woman called Sophy unexpectedly entered the room and recognized Kratides, but Melas was then rushed back to London, after being well paid. Mycroft had advertised for information and received Sophy's address, which is in Beckenham. Meanwhile Melas had been taken to question Kratides further.

Holmes, Watson and Mycroft collect Inspector Gregson and travel to Beckenham, where they find Melas unconscious and Kratides dead from noxious fumes. The latter had been trying to rescue his sister, Sophy, from the influence of Latimer and his colleague, William Kemp, but had been captured by them. They were attempting to force him to sign away rights to his and Sophy's property, and when they failed they had left Kratides and Melas to die as they fled with Sophy. News is later received of the death of the two men under mysterious circumstances in Buda-Pesth.

This case is remarkable for the introduction of the man who has superior deductive powers to those of Holmes, his brother

Mycroft. It is strange that Holmes has never mentioned him before, and even here Holmes does not reveal his actual importance. One is also left to wonder who the mysterious J. Davenport was, who informed Mycroft of Sophy's whereabouts. It is indicated in this case that Holmes may not always have been consistent in his attitudes to knowledge, for he had considered that astronomy was of no use to his profession in *A Study in Scarlet*, but he is able to discuss some rather technical aspects of astronomy in this case. Perhaps he had been involved in a case more recently which required such knowledge.

THE ADVENTURE OF THE NAVAL TREATY

First published: *The Strand Magazine* in November 1893
Main Characters: Percy Phelps, Annie Harrison, Joseph Harrison, Lord Holdhurst

Watson requests Holmes's assistance on behalf of an old school friend, Percy Phelps. At Phelps's house they meet Annie, his fiancée, who has been nursing him. He has suffered brain fever since losing an important naval treaty which he was copying alone in his office at the Foreign Office some ten weeks previously. He had visited the commissionaire's office and while there heard the bell ring from his own office. When he returned to his office the treaty was gone.

Holmes visits Lord Holdhurst, the Foreign Secretary and uncle of Phelps, and deduces that the theft must have been unplanned, since no-one knew that the treaty would be in Phelps's office. Holmes discovers the next day that there has been an attempted burglary in Phelps's sickroom, on the first night that Phelps had slept alone. He pretends to return to London with Phelps and Watson. Actually he returns to 221B the next morning, when Phelps is allowed to discover the missing treaty under a dish cover.

Holmes had caught Annie's brother, Joseph, attempting to recover the treaty from Phelps's sickroom. Joseph had visited Phelps unexpectedly and saw the treaty. He had stolen it to pay debts, and had hidden it in the room in which Phelps had since been sleeping. Although Holmes informs the police about the crime, he allows Harrison time to escape, to avoid scandal in the newspapers.

Holmes has, quite rightly, received a great deal of criticism over an incidental scene which is irrelevant to his analysis of the case. Holmes, in a pensive mood, remarks that the colour and scent of a rose are arbitrary and thus indicate some divine providence. These attributes of a rose are, of course, not pointless, since they attract insects to pollinate the flower. This temporary diversion from Holmes's rationalistic philosophy, however, reveals something of the complexity of his character which he normally strives to conceal.

"WHAT A LOVELY THING A ROSE IS." *Holmes in a rare moment of sentimental philosophizing (above).*

"HOLMES WAS WORKING HARD OVER A CHEMICAL INVESTIGATION." *Watson requests Holmes's expertise in helping an old school chum who has lost a treaty (left).*

THE ADVENTURE OF THE FINAL PROBLEM

First published: *The Strand Magazine* in December 1893
Main Character: Professor Moriarty

"PROFESSOR MORIARTY STOOD BEFORE ME." *The Napoleon of crime (above).*

"THE DEATH OF SHERLOCK HOLMES." *Watson imagines the final struggle that led to the mightly fall of Holmes and Moriarty (far right).*

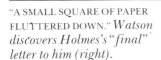

"A SMALL SQUARE OF PAPER FLUTTERED DOWN." *Watson discovers Holmes's "final" letter to him (right).*

Watson attempts to correct rumours about the events which led to the disappearance of Holmes some years previously. Holmes had collected evidence which would lead to the arrest of the Moriarty gang, and to the execution of their leader, "The Napoleon of Crime". Holmes had been threatened by Moriarty and attacked by his agents. He asked Watson to accompany him on a trip to the Continent until the gang has been captured. Moriarty hired a special train to follow the pair, but they evaded him by leaving their Dover boat train and diverting to the Newhaven ferry.

On the Continent they learn that Moriarty had avoided arrest, and they continued their journey to reach Meiringen in Switzerland. Whilst walking near the Reichenbach Falls, Watson was decoyed back to their hotel, and returned to the Falls to find a note from Holmes which explained that Holmes and Moriarty were about to engage in a fight to the death. The signs of the struggle indicated that both men had

plunged over the Falls to their deaths, and Watson returned to England alone.

Conan Doyle intended this to be the very last Holmes story, and it neatly sums up Holmes's dedication to improving his world through the destruction of its worst criminal member. Holmes's ending could hardly be more dramatic, and yet the action is only surmised. The description poignantly reveals Watson's deepest feelings for Holmes and creates a great sense of loss. There are, however, some interesting problems left by the narrative. Watson claims that he has never heard of Moriarty, yet he was very familiar with him only a few years earlier in *The Valley of Fear*. There is also the strange reference to Holmes's fear of air-guns, which is not explained in any way.

THE HOUND OF THE BASKERVILLES

First published: *The Strand Magazine* from August 1901 to April 1902
Main Characters: Dr Mortimer, Sir Charles Baskerville, Sir Henry Baskerville, Barrymore,
Jack Stapleton, Beryl Stapleton, Mr Frankland, Laura Lyons, Inspector Lestrade,
the hound

Doctor Mortimer arrives at Baker Street to inform Holmes and Watson that Sir Charles Baskerville has died of heart failure in mysterious circumstances in the grounds of his Dartmoor home. Mortimer relates the legend of a spectral hound haunting the Baskerville family and he then asks for advice about the next heir, Sir Henry, who is about to arrive from Canada to take up his inheritance. On arrival, Sir Henry receives a cryptic note warning him away from the Moor. At his hotel one of his old boots is stolen.

Holmes sends Watson to accompany Sir Henry to Dartmoor with Doctor Mortimer, and there they find that a convicted murderer, Selden, has escaped from the prison on the Moor. Sir Henry meets a local butterfly collector, Jack Stapleton, and soon

falls in love with Stapleton's sister, Beryl. Sir Henry's butler, Barrymore, is found signalling at night to the convict, and it is revealed that he has been supplying Selden with food because the latter is Barrymore's brother-in-law. Whilst vainly pursuing Selden with Sir Henry, Watson briefly sees a mysterious man standing on one of the Moor's tors.

Barrymore informs Watson that immediately prior to his death, Sir Charles had received a letter from a lady with the initials "LL", asking him to meet her at the gate to the Moor on the night he died. Barrymore also reports that Selden has seen the other man on the Moor. Watson discovers that the lady is Laura Lyons, and he interviews her but finds out little more.

Watson sets out onto the Moor to find the hiding place of "the man on the tor" only to

"HOLDING IT ONLY AN INCH OR TWO FROM HIS EYES." *Holmes examines the letter warning Sir Henry away from the Moor (above).*

EDWARDIAN POSTCARD *(far left) promoting* The Hound of the Baskervilles.

"OVER THE ROCKS WAS THRUST OUT AN EVIL YELLOW FACE." *Watson and Sir Henry disturb the escaped convict on the Moor (left).*

PETER CUSHING AND HIS PIPE *(top and above). The pipe used by the actor in the Hammer Films production of* The Hound of the Baskervilles, *1959.*

discover that it is Holmes, who has been carrying out his own investigations. He has discovered that the murderer is Stapleton, who is married to his "sister" Beryl, and who has promised marriage to Laura Lyons, primarily to gain her assistance in decoying Sir Charles. As darkness falls they hear the cries of someone being pursued by a hound and find a body which appears to be that of Sir Henry. It is actually Selden, who is wearing some of Sir Henry's old clothes. Stapleton soon arrives on the scene, and Holmes informs him that he and Watson have been unsuccessful in their investigations and are to return to London. Holmes and Watson proceed to Baskerville Hall, where Holmes recognizes the likeness of Stapleton in the family portraits and realizes that he is the son of Sir Charles's younger brother who had died, supposedly without issue, in South America. Holmes then persuades Sir Henry to join Stapleton for dinner on the next evening, and to walk back across the Moor to Baskerville Hall.

Holmes and Watson pretend to leave for London, but collect Lestrade from the station before hiding on the Moor outside Stapleton's house. Sir Henry leaves the house and vanishes into the mist just as the hound appears, chasing after Sir Henry. Holmes shoots the dog and discovers that its spectral appearance is due to the effect of phosphorescent paint. Beryl is found tied up in the house and Stapleton disappears into the mist on Grimpen Mire, where he is assumed to have drowned. Sir Henry sets off on a world trip to recover from his attack.

Holmes informs Watson that he had solved the outlines of the crime from deducing that an old boot had been taken in order to provide the hound with a scent, and that the warning note had come from a woman because of the perfume on it. He had traced most of Stapleton's history from the latter's careless revelation to Watson that he had once been a schoolteacher. The rest of the case had merely involved the confirmation of details.

BASIL RATHBONE AND NIGEL BRUCE *in a publicity still for Hollywood's* The Hound of the Baskervilles, *1939.*

This narrative was written after the loss of Holmes at Reichenbach, but deals with an earlier case. It is deservedly the most popular of all the Sherlock Holmes stories, and it contains few major problems, considering the length and complexity of the plot. It does contain some supreme examples of the annoying way in which Holmes prevents Watson, and thereby us, from being able to solve the case, in that he deliberately withholds such information as the faint perfume on the warning note. In addition we

"I SAW THE FIGURE OF A MAN UPON THE TOR." *Despite the bright moonlight Watson is unable to recognize the distinctive figure of his colleague Holmes (far left).*

"THE HOUND OF THE BASKERVILLES." *Not what one would classify as Man's Best Friend (left).*

THE CURSE OF THE BASKERVILLES. *Francis de Wolff as Dr Mortimer relates the legend of the Baskerville hound to Andre Morell and Peter Cushing in the 1959 Hammer production.*

"HOLMES EMPTIED FIVE BARRELS OF HIS REVOLVER INTO THE CREATURE'S FLANK." *Holmes saves Sir Henry from the jaws of death and ends the danger of the phosphorescent hound.*

are not made suspicious of Stapleton, in that we are not made privy to the investigations which Holmes carries out into his background. Perhaps the main difficulty in the plot is the one which Holmes himself does not adequately answer, which is exactly how Stapleton intended taking possession of the estate if his plan to murder Sir Henry had been successful. A solution might involve the use of an agent to claim the estate, as Holmes suggests, with the later removal of that agent, in the same way that Beryl and Laura might have required "removal". One rather unsatisfactory element of the narrative is the way that Sir Henry appears to abandon his love for Beryl, when the latter had done everything she could to help him short of directly betraying her husband. These minor points are more than compensated for by the totally dramatic effect of the narrative. There can be few who do not still feel a sense of excitement when they read such lines as "Mr Holmes, they were the footprints of a gigantic hound!"

THE ADVENTURE OF THE EMPTY HOUSE

First published: *Collier's* in September 1903
Main Characters: Colonel Moran, Ronald Adair, Inspector Lestrade

Watson visits the scene of the murder of Ronald Adair, who has been shot with a bullet from a short-range revolver, in a room locked from the inside. Watson is followed home by an elderly bookseller, who dramatically reveals himself to be Holmes. Holmes explains that he defeated Moriarty three years previously and then climbed a cliff to leave no traces of his escape, although he was seen doing this by Colonel Moran, Moriarty's chief assistant. Holmes has travelled the world, and on returning has become involved in the "Park Lane mystery".

That night, Holmes takes Watson to an empty house opposite 221B, from which they see the silhouette of a bust of Holmes projected onto the curtain of their old flat. Moran enters the empty house and shoots the bust of Holmes with a powerful air-gun, firing a revolver bullet across the street. After arresting Moran, Holmes explains to

Lestrade that Moran had killed Adair in the same way.

This narrative presents many difficulties. Holmes states that he disappeared to confound remaining members of the Moriarty gang, yet Moran was already aware of his survival. Holmes's journey to Tibet would have been almost impossible in those days, and it certainly confused Watson who records in the *Strand* version that Holmes visited the Head Llama, rather than the Head Lama! Also, Holmes could not have visited the Khalifa in Khartoum at that time since the Khalifa left that city in 1885. Perhaps Holmes was engaged in activities which Mycroft would not allow him to reveal even to Watson. The reference to air-guns in *The Final Problem* would have been an excellent link to *The Empty House*, but one must recall that *The Final Problem* had been written as the last Holmes case. In *The Empty House* we discover that both Professor Moriarty and his brother, Colonel Moriarty, have the name of James. This may have been part of their surname, and it is therefore a pity that we are not given the full name of the third Moriarty brother. In spite of its many problems, the case is redeemed by the return of Holmes!

VIEWS OF THE DRAWING ROOM AT 221B *(above and left). The reconstructed room is in the Sherlock Holmes Pub in London.*

"I CREPT FORWARD AND LOOKED ACROSS AT THE FAMILIAR WINDOW." *Standing next to the detective Watson is amazed at the silhouette of Holmes illuminated in the drawing room of 221B across the street.*

THE ADVENTURE OF THE NORWOOD BUILDER

First published: *Collier's* in October 1903
Main Characters: John McFarlane, Jonas Oldacre, Inspector Lestrade

John Hector McFarlane visits 221B hurriedly and informs Holmes that he is about to be arrested for the murder of Jonas Oldacre, immediately before Lestrade arrives to do just that. Oldacre, a builder living in Norwood, had disappeared and McFarlane's bloody walking stick had been found at his home, together with some bones in the ashes of a fire. McFarlane claims that he had been asked to finalize Oldacre's will and had found that Oldacre was leaving everything to him. Oldacre had explained that he had known McFarlane's parents, but that he had no relatives of his own to leave his estate to, and had asked

COLLIER'S THE NORWOOD BUILDER. American illustrator Frederic Dorr Steele's rendition of Holmes. The handprint on the wall is artistic licence. Oldacre used McFarlane's thumb print according to Watson.

McFarlane to visit his house late at night to complete the matter. Holmes discovers that, when young, Oldacre had been rejected as a suitor by McFarlane's mother, and that there are no valuable documents at the house. He also finds that large bank payments had been made recently by Oldacre to a Mr Cornelius.

On being summoned to Oldacre's house by Lestrade to examine a bloody thumb print which is McFarlane's, Holmes informs Watson that it had not been there the day before, yet McFarlane is still in gaol. Holmes then starts a smoky fire in the house, which drives Oldacre out of the hiding place which Holmes had discovered by comparing the internal and external dimensions of the house. McFarlane's print had been obtained by Oldacre from a wax seal, and he had planned the whole affair out of revenge against Mrs McFarlane.

This case sees the introduction of the use of fingerprints as evidence, although it is interesting that this particular thumb print is a false one. We also discover something of the value which Holmes attached to Watson's assistance in the way that he has indirectly bought Watson's practice. Since Holmes was not in favour of publicity, it can be suggested that Watson may well have provided assistance for Holmes which his own modesty prevented him from mentioning, or that he did not wish to diminish the image of Holmes which he was largely responsible for having created.

THE ADVENTURE OF THE DANCING MEN

First published: *The Strand Magazine* in December 1903
Main Characters: Hilton Cubitt, Elsie Cubitt, Abe Slaney

Mr Hilton Cubitt gives Holmes a copy of a series of chalked stickmen figures which had been appearing at his house in Norfolk, and asks him to decipher them. Cubitt had

married Elsie Patrick, an American, who had asked him not to enquire into her past, and she had fainted when shown the first of the figures. Holmes analyses the figures but is unable to travel immediately to Norfolk. He eventually arrives to find that Cubitt and his wife have been shot. The servants had heard a loud explosion from the study, followed by a lesser one, and found Cubitt dead and his wife wounded, with a pistol containing two empty chambers. Holmes finds a third bullet embedded in the edge of a window, with the empty case outside.

Holmes then sends a note to a nearby farm, and explains that the figures are an alphabetical substitution code which he had solved by letter-frequency analysis. His note, using this code, had invited the originator of the messages, Abe Slaney, to visit Elsie. Slaney is arrested on arrival and confesses that he had been a member of a gang run by Elsie's father, the inventor of the code. He had been engaged to her, but she had left America when he would not give up crime. Slaney had met Elsie in the study and been surprised by Cubitt. They had exchanged shots, Slaney's causing Cubitt's fatal wound, and this had been heard as one loud explosion. Elsie had attempted suicide, causing the second explosion, but she later recovers. Holmes had deduced most of this from the amount of gun smoke which had been noted in the study.

This is another of Holmes's unsatisfactory cases, since he loses his client through being unable to travel to Norfolk overnight. In spite of the possibility of hiring special trains, this is a reminder that overnight, or even late-night, trains were not very common in England during the age of Victoria. The code used in this case is an extremely simple one, and it is therefore unfortunate that those who attempt to emulate Holmes's breaking of the code will find it rather difficult to do so, for most versions of the case have mistakes introduced by the printers, and these mistakes vary according to the printer. The fact that Holmes was keeping Watson's cheque book is possibly a reminder that Watson was inclined to spend too much of his pension on horseracing.

"HOLMES CLAPPED A PISTOL TO HIS HEAD AND MARTIN SLIPPED THE HANDCUFFS OVER HIS WRISTS." *The sleuth traps the not-so-honest Abe.*

THE DANCING MEN. *Part of the uncompleted message. Deciphered, it reads:* "at Elri".

THE ADVENTURE OF THE SOLITARY CYCLIST

First published: *Collier's* in December 1903
Main Characters: Violet Smith, Bob Carruthers, Jack Woodley, Mr Williamson

"AS WE APPROACHED, THE LADY STAGGERED AGAINST THE TRUNK OF THE TREE." Rescued from an unsavoury marriage.

"HOLMES TOSSED THE END OF HIS CIGARETTE INTO THE GRATE." Perhaps an ashtray was too much to ask (below).

Violet Smith informs Holmes that in response to a newspaper advertisement she and her mother had contacted a Mr Carruthers and a Mr Woodley, who told them that their last relative, Violet's uncle, had died penniless in South Africa, but that he had asked them to care for his relatives. Carruthers offers Violet employment, living at his home near Farnham. At the house, Woodley had attempted to force his attentions on Violet and had been forcibly ejected by Carruthers. As Violet cycled to the station each weekend after this she noted that she was being followed by a bearded cyclist.

Watson investigates and sees a cyclist vanish into the grounds of a house rented by a Mr Williamson. Holmes discovers that Williamson is possibly a defrocked priest. Carruthers proposes to Violet, which prompts her decision to leave. Holmes and Watson

travel to meet her and are joined by the bearded cyclist, who turns out to be Carruthers, then find that she has just been forcibly "married" by Williamson (an unfrocked priest) to Woodley. Carruthers shoots Woodley and wounds him.

It is revealed that Carruthers and Woodley knew that Violet's uncle was rich and about to die, and they had sought out his only two relatives: Woodley won at cards the "right" to marry Violet, but Carruthers fell in love with her and tried to protect her. Woodley and Williamson are imprisoned.

There is some confusion as to who the solitary cyclist is. Since Violet is the most important cyclist it might be thought to be her, and Watson's introduction appears to indicate this, but Carruthers is specifically referred to as a solitary cyclist later in the case. It would be very difficult to explain why Woodley bothered obtaining a marriage licence, since the "wedding" is illegal on several other grounds. The editor of *The Strand Magazine* rejected the first draft of this case because Holmes did not appear to have had enough to do, which may account for Watson recording Holmes's criticisms of himself so strongly.

THE ADVENTURE OF THE PRIORY SCHOOL

First published: *Collier's* in January 1904
Main Characters: Dr Thorneycroft Huxtable, the Duke of Holdernesse, Lord Saltire,
Heidegger, James Wilder, Reuben Hayes

Dr Huxtable, the headmaster of the Priory School, explains that Lord Saltire, the son of the Duke of Holdernesse, has disappeared from his school in the Peak District. A German master, Heidegger, is also missing. Holmes and Watson return with Huxtable to the school. The Duke's secretary, James Wilder, rebukes Huxtable for involving outside assistance, but then the Duke reluctantly asks for Holmes's help. Following bicycle tracks amongst the cow tracks on the moors, Holmes finds Heidegger's body, and then continues to the Fighting Cock inn, where the owner, Reuben Hayes, although uncooperative, reveals that he had once been dismissed from the service of the Duke.

After realizing that he had seen no cows on the moors, Holmes deduces that Lord Saltire must have been abducted using a horse with cowprint shoes, and he notices that Hayes's horses have new shoes. Leaving the inn, Holmes sees Wilder arrive there on a bicycle with the same tread as the one on the moors. Hayes then flees. Holmes confronts the Duke with knowing that his son has been abducted by Wilder, and the Duke reveals that Wilder is his illegitimate son. Holmes announces that he has arranged the arrest of Hayes, and Lord Saltire is retrieved from the inn. The Duke states that Wilder will leave for Australia. Holmes permits this, even though Wilder is the instigator of the kidnapping of Lord Saltire and the murder of Heidegger by Hayes on the moors.

There is some discussion as to whether the Duke attempts to bribe Holmes, and whether the latter actually accepts such an offer, for the reward appears to double. Watson's Literary Agent had to admit some incorrect interference in the narrative, when he discovered that one cannot determine the direction of travel of a bicycle in the way described. Holmes obviously used other signs to assist his deduction, but, as often happened, Watson possibly did not record all of them. This case involves an extreme example of Holmes by-passing the due process of law without, however, his usual moral justification.

"I HEARD HIM CHUCKLE AS THE LIGHT FELL UPON A PATCHED DUNLOP TYRE." *Holmes begins to deflate the murder mystery (far left).*

"THERE LAY THE UNFORTUNATE RIDER." *Holmes and Watson find the body of Heidegger.*

THE ADVENTURE OF BLACK PETER

First published: *Collier's* in February 1904
Main Characters: Inspector Hopkins, Peter Carey, John Neligan, Patrick Cairns

Holmes informs Watson that he has vainly spent the early morning attempting to pierce a pig's carcase with a harpoon. Inspector Hopkins relates that Captain "Black Peter" Carey, a retired whaler, had been found harpooned to the wall in his garden hut. On visiting the hut, Holmes, Watson and Hopkins find that someone has attempted to gain entry since the murder. When the intruder returns he is found to be John Hopley Neligan, the son of a banker who had failed in business, fled in a small yacht across the North Sea, then vanished. Some of the shares he had been carrying had recently come onto the market, and Neligan had traced them to Carey, and he claims that he was trying to discover more about his father from Carey's logbooks.

Hopkins arrests Neligan. Holmes advertises for a harpooner, and when a Patrick Cairns visits Holmes for the job he is arrested by Holmes. Neligan senior had been rescued by Carey's boat, but Cairns had seen Carey throw Neligan into the sea after robbing him of the shares he was carrying. Cairns had visited Carey and killed him during a quarrel over sharing the ill-gotten gains. Holmes had deduced that the killer was a harpooner from a sealskin pouch found in the hut, from the rum on a table, and from the strength and skill needed to pierce a man with a harpoon.

Once again, this is a classic example of Holmes examining the relevant information where others cling to only the more obvious evidence. Hopkins is quite correct when he warns John Neligan that he should keep the rest of his statement for the courts, for police officials at that time were specifically ordered not to take statements from those who might be accused. This, of course, constantly places Holmes at an advantage over those officials who obey this particular regulation, although there are numerous examples of it being ignored.

THE ADVENTURE OF CHARLES AUGUSTUS MILVERTON

First published: *Collier's* in March 1904
Main Characters: Lady Eva Brackwell, Charles Augustus Milverton, Agatha, Inspector Lestrade

Holmes is asked by Lady Brackwell to retrieve some imprudent letters from Charles Augustus Milverton, an infamous blackmailer. Milverton refuses Holmes's offer of a reduced settlement, and Holmes then obtains information about Milverton's house by becoming engaged to Milverton's maid, Agatha. With Watson he burgles the house, but they have to hide when Milverton arrives to interview a maid who wishes to sell some letters. The "maid" is found to be a lady whose husband killed himself after Milverton revealed her indiscretions.

The lady shoots Milverton dead and flees. Holmes destroys the material in Milverton's safe before he and Watson narrowly escape. Lestrade asks Holmes for assistance but Holmes refuses on the grounds that some crimes deserve to go unpunished. Holmes later identifies the lady to Watson.

There are numerous moral problems in this case. Firstly Holmes and Watson commit the crime of burglary, then Holmes destroys private property from Milverton's safe. Holmes condones a murder, and re-

fuses to help the police, even when he discovers who the murderer is. Even Watson threatens Holmes, indicating that he will report Holmes for burglary if he does not allow Watson to help. Perhaps Holmes's worst "crime", however, is the way in which he uses the maid, Agatha, to satisfy his own requirements. The case does contain an excellent example of Holmes's humour, though, when he points out to Inspector Lestrade that the description of one of the men seen leaving the scene of the murder fits that of Watson.

HUBERT WILLIS AND EILLE NORWOOD. *Norwood as Holmes shows Willis as Watson the key to the case in the 1922 film of* Charles Augustus Milverton.

"EXHIBITING THE BUTT OF A LARGE REVOLVER, WHICH PROJECTED FROM THE INSIDE POCKET." *Milverton makes his exit (above left).*

"THEN HE STAGGERED TO HIS FEET AND RECEIVED ANOTHER SHOT." *Milverton gets more than he blackmailed for (far left).*

"FOLLOWING HIS GAZE I SAW THE PICTURE OF A REGAL AND STATELY LADY IN COURT DRESS." *Holmes identifies the woman who ended the corrupt Milverton's life.*

THE ADVENTURE OF THE SIX NAPOLEONS

First published: *Collier's* in April 1904
Main Characters: Inspector Lestrade, Beppo, Pietro Venucci

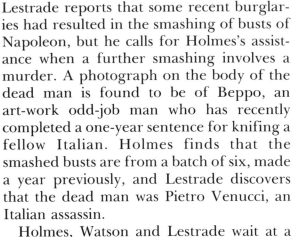

Lestrade reports that some recent burglaries had resulted in the smashing of busts of Napoleon, but he calls for Holmes's assistance when a further smashing involves a murder. A photograph on the body of the dead man is found to be of Beppo, an art-work odd-job man who has recently completed a one-year sentence for knifing a fellow Italian. Holmes finds that the smashed busts are from a batch of six, made a year previously, and Lestrade discovers that the dead man was Pietro Venucci, an Italian assassin.

Holmes, Watson and Lestrade wait at a house where one of the two remaining busts is located and arrest a burglar who smashes the bust. Holmes then buys the last bust and smashes it to find the black pearl of the Borgias inside. Beppo had stuck the pearl in the still-wet bust at the manufacturers where he worked, prior to being arrested for the knifing. Venucci had possibly been connected with the original theft of the pearl and had been killed in a struggle when Beppo had obtained that particular bust.

Holmes appears to take a very serious risk in this case when he chooses which house to wait at for Beppo. He might at least have had Lestrade guard the other house. It is also difficult to explain why Holmes has the owner of the final bust sign all rights of possession to him, as neither of them has any right to the pearl. Perhaps Holmes did not want the owner to realize the real value of the bust, in terms of a possible reward.

THE ADVENTURE OF THE THREE STUDENTS

First published: *The Strand Magazine* in June 1904
Main Characters: Hilton Soames, Bannister, Gilchrist

Whilst carrying out some private researches at a university, Holmes is asked by Hilton Soames, a tutor, to investigate the compromising of a Greek examination paper. Soames had returned to his rooms to find a key in the door, the paper moved, some pencil sharpenings and a scratch on the writing desk. His servant, Bannister, had carelessly left the key in the door, and had almost fainted when shown the paper. Holmes sees that the room has very high-set windows, and finds some pellets of dark clay and sawdust in the room. He deduces that the intruder had been there for about a quarter of an hour.

There are three students living above the room who are suspect, and after investigating these and some locations in the town, Holmes accuses Bannister of finding the culprit and concealing him in Soames's bedroom until the coast was clear. One of the students, Gilchrist, is called and confesses. Holmes had deduced the culprit from his height, which had enabled him to see the paper through the high window, and that the pellets came from a long-jump pit, with the scratch being caused by Gilchrist's spiked shoes. Bannister had not almost fainted, but sat down to hide Gilchrist's gloves. Bannister had been butler to Gilchrist's father and wished to help him. Gilchrist had already decided not to take the examination, but to leave for service with the Rhodesian Police.

This is an extremely important case in connection with the discussion of Holmes's own university. It provides many clues but some of these are contradictory. Holmes is obviously familiar with this town, as opposed to the Cambridge of *The Missing Three-Quarter*. The expression "quadrangle" is used, which suggests Oxford, as opposed to the use of "court" at Cambridge. The black clay for jumping pits, however, is a mark of the Cambridge of that time. It has been pointed out that not only are the chapters in Thucydides too short for half a chapter to take so long to copy, but that a cheat would need only to note the beginning and the end of an extract from such a well-known work.

THE ADVENTURE OF THE GOLDEN PINCE-NEZ

First published: *The Strand Magazine* in July 1904
Main Characters: Inspector Hopkins, Professor Coram, Anna

Inspector Hopkins informs Holmes that he has been investigating the death of Professor Coram's secretary, Willoughby Smith. A scream had been heard and Smith was found bleeding from the neck; his last words were to tell the professor that " – it was she". No-one had been found, although all the exits from the house were blocked. In Smith's hand there was a pair of golden pince-nez. Holmes examines these and produces a detailed description of the owner, a lady. The next day Holmes visits the house and smokes several cigarettes in the bedroom where the professor spends almost all of his time. Holmes leaves the room, then on his return is able to reveal the owner of the pince-nez hiding in the room, having noted her foot marks in the cigarette ash which he had scattered.

The woman is Anna, a Russian Nihilist and Coram's estranged wife, whom he had betrayed in Russia. After her release she had travelled to England and had broken into Coram's house to obtain papers to free her lover back in Russia, when she was then discovered by Smith. They struggled, he grabbed her pince-nez and she stabbed Smith in the neck. Without her pince-nez Anna had accidentally run into Coram's room while trying to escape, and Coram had hidden Anna to prevent his past from being revealed. The secretary's last words

"THE BODY WAS FOUND NEAR THE BUREAU, AND JUST TO THE LEFT OF IT, AS MARKED UPON THAT CHART." Inspector Hopkins shows Holmes where the body of the unfortunate secretary lay.

Holmes, by pretending to be the spy, tempts the man who stole the plans into a rendezvous. The thief is found to be the brother of Sir James, Colonel Valentine Walker. He had taken impressions of his brother's keys for the spy, Herr Oberstein, to pay off debts. Oberstein is similarly lured to the house and the plans are recovered. Soon after this, Holmes visits Windsor, where he obtains an emerald tie-pin from "a certain gracious lady"!

This is one of the most political of the Holmes cases, with references to inter-national spying and the concealed diversion of governmental funds. It also shows an awareness of submarine developments, although these were at an early stage at that time, and the two Holmeses shared this interest with Watson's Literary Agent. It is rather strange that Mycroft has to produce a list of spies, since Sherlock was very famil-iar with them only a few years earlier in *The Second Stain* when his list included Ober-stein. It appears that international negotia-tions may have intruded in the sentencing of Oberstein, for he receives only fifteen years.

"HE SPRANG FORWARD WITH CLENCHED HANDS TOWARDS MY COMPANION." *Sterndale meets his match in Holmes.*

"WE LURCHED THROUGH THE DOOR, AND AN INSTANT AFTERWARDS HAD THROWN OURSELVES DOWN UPON THE GRASS PLOT." *The detectives escape the Devil's Foot poison. Illustrated by Gilbert Holiday.*

THE ADVENTURE OF THE DEVIL'S FOOT

First published: *The Strand Magazine* in December 1910
Main Characters: Mr Roundhay, Mortimer Tregennis, Owen Tregennis, Brenda Tregennis, Leon Sterndale

Ill health forces Holmes to rest in Cornwall with Watson, and there they are visited by the local vicar, Mr Roundhay, and his lod-ger, Mortimer Tregennis. The latter had left his two brothers Owen and George, and his sister Brenda, playing cards at their home the previous night. In the morning they had been found still at the table; the brothers demented and the sister dead. After examining the house Holmes is vis-ited by another local resident Leon Stern-dale, the famous explorer, who has can-celled a trip to Africa over the tragedy. Mortimer Tregennis then dies of the same symptoms as his sister.

Holmes finds some white powder on the top of a lamp, and when he burns some of this on an identical lamp, he and Watson are almost poisoned. Holmes deduces that Mortimer had caused the first poisonings, because of a family quarrel, but had then been poisoned himself by Sterndale when he discovered that Mortimer had taken the Devil's Foot poison from him. Sterndale had loved Brenda, and had thus returned to avenge her death. Holmes allows Stern-dale to leave for work in Africa.

A great deal of interest has been produced in this case with Watson's reference to Hol-mes's "occasional indiscretions", which had possibly aggravated his illness from over-work. There have been suggestions that this may indicate further drug abuse by Holmes at a later stage in his career. It may also have been a reference to Holmes's overuse of tobacco, since this is referred to on several occasions during the case and therefore seems to have been a preoccupation of Watson. Possibly this was the result of some new-fangled medical opinions which implied that smoking was connected with ill health!

THE STRAND MAGAZINE. Cover for the December 1911 issue containing The Disappearance of Lady Frances Carfax. *The story was illustrated by Alec Ball.*

later found in Brixton where a funeral is being arranged. Holmes forces his way into Peters' house and finds a dead, elderly lady in the coffin before he is ejected by the police. Immediately before the funeral, Holmes and Watson force open the coffin and find Lady Frances drugged on top of the old lady. Holmes had deduced this situation from the great depth of the coffin for such a small lady. Lestrade arrives late with a warrant to find that Peters has escaped in the confusion.

The initial deductions which Holmes makes in this case are amongst the most dubious he ever makes, for there are numerous alternative possibilities available. The case is also an extreme example of the contorted means which some villains will choose to commit murder. The ethical distinctions which Holmes outlines over the drugging are certainly rather weak. The conclusion almost suggests that Holmes was pleased to have a Moriarty substitute still at large to provide future challenges.

THE ADVENTURE OF THE DYING DETECTIVE

First published: *The Strand Magazine* in November 1913
Main Characters: Mrs Hudson, Culverton Smith, Victor Savage, Inspector Morton

Mrs Hudson calls Watson to 221B where she claims that Holmes is dying. Watson finds Holmes gaunt, feverish and occasionally delirious from a disease which he says he has caught from some Chinese sailors. He asks Watson to bring a non-medical expert on the disease, Mr Culverton Smith, to him, but to return alone and ahead of Smith. Smith is reluctant, but agrees when he hears that Holmes is delirious. Watson returns to 221B and Holmes asks him to hide behind the bed. Smith arrives and reveals that he is the cause of Holmes's disease, having sent Holmes a box with a poisoned sharp spring on which Holmes had cut himself. Smith admits that he had done this after finding that Holmes knew too much of the way in which he had killed a Victor Savage. Holmes suddenly revives and Inspector Morton arrives to

arrest Smith for the murder of Savage. Smith denies admitting anything to Holmes, but Watson then emerges to conclude the case.

The way in which Holmes convinces Watson that he is delirious is both entertaining and inventive, with his ravings of the world being taken over by oysters. With Holmes's constant concern for those who are ill-treated, he may well have harboured a desire for revenge against the walruses of this world from having read a book which was very popular when he was at college. On a more practical point, it must have been extremely difficult for Watson to have remained hidden behind the bed, and for him to have resisted the urge to rescue Holmes when the latter was being attacked by Smith.

THE VALLEY OF FEAR

First published: *The Strand Magazine* from September 1914 until May 1915
Main Characters: John Douglas, Inspector MacDonald, Professor James Moriarty, Cecil Barker, Mrs Douglas, Hargrave, Ted Baldwin, Bodymaster McGinty, John or "Jack" McMurdo, Ettie Shafter, Birdy Edwards

Holmes receives and decodes a message which implies danger to a John Douglas, whereupon Inspector MacDonald arrives to seek assistance in solving the murder of John Douglas of Birlestone Manor. Holmes suspects that Professor Moriarty is behind the crime, and he travels to Sussex to investigate. Beside the body, the head of which has been blown off with a shotgun, there is a card with "VV 341" on it, and the man's wedding ring has been removed. Douglas had spent many years in America, where he acquired a tattoo on his arm. He had met another Englishman there, Cecil Barker, who was staying with Douglas at the time of the murder.

Barker explains that he heard a single shot, but the only signs of intruders were a footprint on a windowsill and a bicycle abandoned outside the house. Barker suggests that Douglas had been involved with a secret society in America, and mentions that some men had come looking for him soon after he arrived in England. Douglas was always armed, but on the fatal night had left his revolver upstairs. Mrs Douglas states that her husband had lived in dread of a place called the Valley of Fear, and that in a fever he had once called out the name of Bodymaster McGinty. Holmes confounds MacDonald and the local policeman by showing that the slipper worn by Barker exactly fits the footprint on the windowsill.

Watson shortly afterwards sees Mrs Douglas and Barker happily together. Holmes informs Watson that the whole case hangs upon a missing dumb-bell, only one having been found at the scene of the crime, and that he is aware that the stories of Barker and Mrs Douglas are false. The police trace the bicycle to a Mr Hargrave, an American who has disappeared from his nearby hotel. Holmes announces that he is to spend part of the night in the study, and asks MacDonald to inform Barker that he intends having the moat around the house drained. Barker is then seen pulling some

clothes from the moat, weighed down by the missing dumb-bell, and marked "Vermissa, USA". These are found to belong to Hargrave's.

Holmes announces that Douglas is not dead, but hiding in the house, and the body is that of his intended assailant, Hargrave. Douglas emerges to describe how he had fought "Hargrave", whose real name was Ted Baldwin, and killed him. Douglas and Barker had used the lodge tattoo on Baldwin's arm, identical to that of Douglas, to pretend that Baldwin was Douglas. Douglas

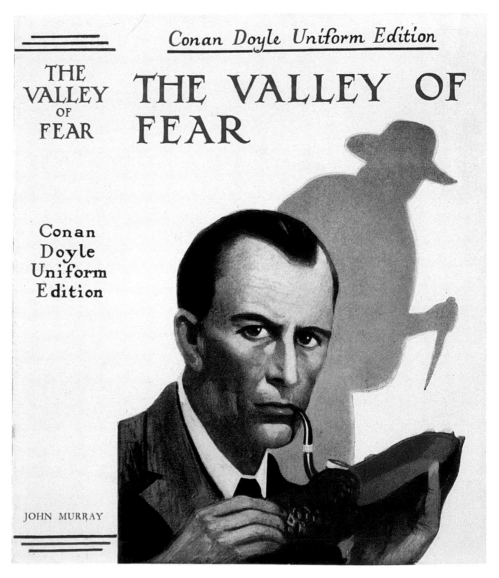

DUST WRAPPER OF UNIFORM BOOK EDITION. *On this 'Thirties cover Holmes is examining a clue to the murder of John Douglas, not trying on a new shoe.*

was unable to remove his own wedding ring: hence its absence from the body.

Watson provides an account of events in the Vermissa Valley in America some twenty years earlier, involving a criminally active lodge of a secret sect. The members of this lodge, the "Vermissa Valley – Lodge Number 341" of the "VV 341" card found near Baldwin's body, were known locally as the Scowrers, and they terrorized the inhabitants of the valley. Douglas, a criminal fugitive then known as John or "Jack" McMurdo, joined the lodge, which was run by McGinty. He then fell in love with Ettie Shafter, already promised against her will to Ted Baldwin. McMurdo was soon accepted by the lodge and made privy to all their evil activities. News reached the lodge that Birdy Edwards, a Pinkerton detective, was on their trail and McMurdo was ordered to set a trap for him. When all the leaders of the Scowrers were in one place, McMurdo revealed that he was Birdy Edwards. He had the place surrounded by police and had enough evidence to hang them all. Edwards left the valley with Ettie and her father, but several members of the gang escaped the police and began to hunt for him. He had married Ettie but she later died, and under the name of John Douglas he had moved to England and remarried.

Douglas is acquitted of the murder of Baldwin, but Holmes advises him to leave England, as he believes that Moriarty has been asked to arrange Douglas's death for the remnants of the Scowrers. Two months later Barker informs Holmes that Douglas was lost overboard from a boat travelling to South Africa. Holmes is convinced that it was murder, and that Moriarty's agents were responsible.

In this novel-length case we find Watson once again returning to his predisposition to supply a great deal of information on a wide variety of topics. As with *A Study in Scarlet* and *The Sign of Four*, he provides an excessive amount of detail on what is, after all, only the background to a Holmesian case. In this habit he would, no doubt, have been fully supported by his Literary Agent, who suffered from the same problem. The case itself is a relatively simple one, but it is given far greater depth and significance because of Holmes's perception of the involvement of Moriarty. The information on Moriarty does present difficulties, however, when in the later case of *The Final Problem* Watson says that he knows nothing of Moriarty. It has been claimed by many interested in psychology and, unfortunately, by Holmesian scholars who should know better, that Moriarty may never actually have existed other than in Holmes's mind. It is often claimed, for example, that only Holmes ever sees Moriarty, and in *The Final Problem* this could be accepted. In *The Valley of Fear*, however, Inspector MacDonald actually meets Moriarty, and it is the way in which the professor charms the policeman that should convince us of his cleverness. At the start of this case we also have the statement by Watson that eventually comes close to being realized, when he hopes that he will one day be there to see Holmes and Moriarty have their day.

HIS LAST BOW

First published: *The Strand Magazine* in September 1917
Main Characters: Von Bork, Von Herling, Altamont

In August 1914, Von Bork, the chief German spy in England, meets with Von Herling, the head of the German legation, prior to the former's return to Germany with details of British defences. Von Bork's plans require only information on British naval signalling systems for completion, and these are about to be delivered by Von Bork's best agent, Altamont, a disaffected Irish-American. The latter arrives after the departure of Von Herling for London. Von Bork is tricked into boastingly revealing the combination of his safe before Altamont hands over the naval codes in a package. Von Bork discovers that this package actually contains a copy of Holmes's book, *A Practical Handbook of Bee-Keeping*, just as Altamont chloroforms him. It is then revealed that Altamont is Holmes, and that the chauffeur who delivered him is Watson.

Holmes has spent two years building up his character of Altamont and then feeding Von Bork useless information, whilst arranging the arrest of Von Bork's other agents. Before taking Von Bork to Scotland Yard, Holmes suggests to Watson that this occasion might be their last chance for a quiet talk, and gives a memorable description of the near future and its ultimately better aftermath.

This, chronologically, is the last recorded case of Holmes and Watson. The partnership is well concluded, with Watson rushing to the assistance of his old colleague, in spite of many years of separation, and with Holmes aptly describing Watson as "the one fixed point in a changing age". A question has been raised as to the authorship of this narrative, since it is written in the third person, as opposed to the majority written by Watson. Watson provides us with the answer in *The Problem of Thor Bridge*, where he records that he played so little part in some cases that they must be written "as by a third person".

"HE WAS GRIPPED AT THE BACK OF HIS NECK BY A GRASP OF IRON, AND A CHLOROFORMED SPONGE WAS HELD IN FRONT OF HIS WRITHING FACE." *A disguised Holmes silences the unsuspecting spy before he has a chance to criticize his* Practical Handbook of Bee-Keeping. *Illustrated by Albert Gilbert.*

THE ADVENTURE OF THE MAZARIN STONE

First published: *The Strand Magazine* in October 1921
Main Characters: the Prime Minister, the Home Secretary, Lord Cantlemere, Count Negretto Silvius, Sam Merton

On returning to Baker Street after a long absence, Watson finds that Holmes has been visited by the Prime Minister, the Home Secretary and Lord Cantlemere, who are concerned about the theft of the great yellow Mazarin stone, a Crown diamond. Holmes informs Watson that the stone has been stolen by Count Negretto Silvius, aided by an ex-boxer, Sam Merton.

Holmes sets up a dummy bust of himself in the window, to decoy any murderous attempts on his life. When Silvius calls at 221B, Watson is sent to fetch the police, but Holmes then also calls in Merton from the street. Holmes tells Silvius all the evidence which he has accumulated against him, then leaves them alone in the room while he pretends to play his violin in the next room.

THE ADVENTURE OF THE THREE GARRIDEBS

First published: *Collier's* in October 1924
Main Characters: John Garrideb, Alexander Garrideb, Nathan Garrideb, Howard Garrideb, "Killer" Evans

COVER FOR *THE STRAND MAGAZINE. The January 1925 issue (right) containing* The Adventure of the Three Garridebs.

"WELL, WE SHALL BE ROUND ABOUT SIX. DR. WATSON WILL COME WITH ME." *Holmes making use of the relatively new invention, the telephone. Illustrated by H.K. Elcock*

John Garrideb informs Holmes that Alexander Garrideb, an American millionaire, had died and left his estate to be divided between any three male Garridebs. None had been found in America, but Nathan Garrideb had been located in London, and it was the latter who wished to bring Holmes into the search. Holmes visits Nathan, who wishes him to find a third Garrideb. John Garrideb then announces that he has found a third, Howard Garrideb, from an advertisement issued in Birmingham. John asks Nathan to go to Birmingham to obtain an affidavit from Howard.

Holmes and Watson conceal themselves in Nathan's house whilst he is away, and they see John arrive and enter a secret chamber under the floor where counterfeiting equipment is revealed to be hidden. Holmes knocks him out. John, whose real name is "Killer" Evans, had decoyed Nathan away to get at the equipment of a former criminal colleague.

Here we have the use of a telephone at 221B, although there had been earlier references to telephones. It is also in this case that Watson records that Holmes had declined a knighthood. In *The Bruce-Partington Plans* and other cases he does state that he is not interested in honours, but in *The Golden Pince-Nez* it was noted that he had accepted the Legion of Honour. All those who hold this award are Chevaliers of

the Order, and thus might technically be considered knights. As a Chevalier, might Holmes, when visiting Miss Adler's (*A Scandel in Bohemia*) district, have been tempted to sing: "Every little scene, seems to whisper Irene"?

THE ADVENTURE OF THE ILLUSTRIOUS CLIENT

First published: *The Strand Magazine* in November 1924
Main Characters: Colonel Sir James Damery, General de Merville, Violet de Merville, Baron Gruner, Shinwell Johnson, Kitty Winter

Colonel Sir James Damery reluctantly informs Holmes that he is acting on behalf of an anonymous benefactor who wishes to help General de Merville in a matter of personal urgency. Holmes is employed to prevent the general's daughter, Violet, from marrying the Austrian murderer, Baron Gruner. Holmes informs Gruner that he does intend to prevent the wedding, and is threatened in return. One of Holmes's agents, a reformed ex-convict called Shinwell Johnson, introduces Holmes to Kitty Winter, who seeks revenge against Gruner for being abandoned by him after an affair. She informs Holmes that Gruner keeps a book listing his female conquests.

Holmes and Kitty attempt to persuade Violet against Gruner, but she is so infatuated that she will not believe accounts of his previous ill-treatment of women. Holmes is then attacked, but feigns worse injuries. Watson is sent to Gruner's house to divert him with an offer of a Ming saucer for his collection. Holmes takes Kitty to help him find Gruner's book, but she throws acid in Gruner's face, blinding and disfiguring him. Kitty receives a minimal sentence and Violet ends the affair.

In this case Holmes reveals some important clues about his attitudes towards women. It is strange that he does not force the full disclosure of the identity of the "illustrious client" who actually has made Damery present the case to Holmes. There are indications that this might have been Edward VII himself. This case has some peculiar inclusions. Why, for example, does Holmes have his jacket with him in the Turkish Bath?

THE ADVENTURE OF THE THREE GABLES

First published: *Liberty* in September 1926
Main Characters: Steve Dixie, Barney Stockdale, Mary Maberley, Susan, Douglas Maberley, Langdale Pike, Isadora Klein, the Duke of Lomond

Holmes is dramatically threatened not to intrude in affairs at Harrow by Steve Dixie, a negro boxer, supposedly on the orders of Barney Stockdale. Holmes intimidates Dixie with his knowledge of the latter's criminal activities. Mrs Maberley of Harrow had already asked Holmes to investigate the suspiciously high price she had been offered for her house, provided that she leaves most of the contents of the house within it. When Holmes discovers that Mrs Maberley's maid, Susan, has been spying on her, the latter leaves the household immediately. Mrs Maberley's son, Douglas, had died of pneumonia in Rome the previous month, and some of his papers are taken when the house is burgled, although one page, revealing that it had been part of a dramatic novel, had accidentally dropped out on to the floor.

Holmes discovers from Langdale Pike, a well-known social gossip-monger, that Douglas had been the lover of Isadora Klein, an extremely wealthy and beautiful widow who is about to marry the young Duke of Lomond. Isadora reluctantly admits to Holmes that after she had eventually rejected Douglas, he had written a novel about their affair and had sent her one of the two copies to let her know of the contents. She had been attempting to obtain the other copy by buying the house containing it. Holmes allows her to keep the other copy in exchange for a trip around the world for Mrs Maberley.

This case has generated a great deal of comment about Holmes's seemingly racial attitude to Steve Dixie. Although all claims of prejudice can be explained away, it is difficult to excuse the natural interpretation. Although he suggests that Dixie is compounding a felony, as he himself does in several other cases, Dixie is not actually guilty of that crime, but of "misprision of felony", the concealing of a felony.

THE ADVENTURE OF THE BLANCHED SOLDIER

First published: *Liberty* in October 1926
Main Characters: James Dodd, Godfrey Emsworth, Colonel Emsworth, Mrs Emsworth, Sir James Saunders

James Dodd informs Holmes that his Army friend, Godfrey Emsworth, had been wounded in South Africa, and that only vague information could be obtained about the present location of Godfrey from his father, Colonel Emsworth. After visiting Godfrey's mother, Dodd had caught a glimpse of Godfrey, who was looking very blanched in colour and appeared to be restrained in a small house in the grounds of the Emsworth estate.

Holmes visits Colonel Emsworth with Dodd and an anonymous accomplice, and informs him that he knows why Godfrey is being hidden. He passes the Colonel a note with the single word "leprosy" on it, and Godfrey is brought to the house. After being wounded he had unknowingly slept in a leper hospital, and then developed the symptoms when he returned to England. Holmes's companion, Sir James Saunders, is an expert on the disease, and he diagnoses that Godfrey has the non-contagious disease of pseudo-leprosy.

"HE SPRANG BACK WHEN HE SAW THAT I WAS LOOKING AT HIM AND VANISHED INTO THE DARKNESS." In this story, recorded by Holmes, James Dodd explains how he was startled by the pale figure of his lost friend Godfrey.

This is one of the two cases which Holmes records himself, and Watson plays no active part in it. It will be seen that it is very much in the same style as that of Watson, in spite of Holmes's frequent criticisms of that style elsewhere. Holmes also has to admit that Watson's absence presents him with difficulties in narrating the case. It appears too that Holmes suffers from the same problem as Watson in connection with his remembrance of railway journeys, for he claims that he set off for Bedford from Euston, when the London terminus for that town is St Pancras. The case has a key reference to the possibility of a second wife for Watson.

THE ADVENTURE OF THE LION'S MANE

First published: *Liberty* in November 1926
Main Characters: Harold Stackhurst, Fitzroy McPherson, Ian Murdoch, Maud Bellamy, Inspector Bardle

This narrative is recorded by Holmes himself, and Watson plays no active part in it. Holmes relates how, whilst walking from his retirement home on the South Downs to the beach, he had met Harold Stackhurst, a local headmaster. They discovered Fitzroy McPherson, another teacher from Stackhurst's establishment, who was wearing a swimming costume and was covered in whip-like marks. McPherson muttered "the lion's mane" and then died. Ian Murdoch, another teacher, arrived and behaved in a rather suspicious manner. Holmes and Stackhurst visited Maud Bellamy, McPherson's fiancée, but she was unable to help.

Stackhurst dismissed Murdoch from his school because he would not divulge information which he appeared to have in connection with the mystery. A week later, McPherson's dog is found dead near where his master died. Inspector Bardle suggested that Murdoch should be arrested, but as Holmes was explaining that there was in fact no case against him, the very man arrived, covered in marks like those of McPherson. Holmes showed Bardle and Stackhurst that the "murderer" was a poisonous jellyfish which looks like a lion's mane. Murdoch had survived the attack because he was fitter, and he explained that he had appeared to behave suspiciously because he did not wish to reveal that he had loved Maud Bellamy.

Holmes appears to contradict one of his earliest statements about himself here. In *A Study in Scarlet* he had stated that only a fool stored every piece of information in the attic of his brain, whereas here he states that his brain is like a crowded box-room. What he does not explain is how he differentiates between the trifles which might be useful later, and those which might not. At the conclusion of the case he quite rightly criticizes himself, but for the wrong reason. He states that the unused towel misled him into believing that McPherson had not been in the water. Immediately after McPherson's death, however, he correctly deduced that McPherson had either not been in the water or had not bothered drying himself. It was this second option which Holmes forgot.

THE ADVENTURE OF THE RETIRED COLOURMAN

First published: *Liberty* in December 1926
Main Characters: Josiah Amberley, Mrs Amberley, Dr Ray Ernest, Inspector McKinnon

Josiah Amberley, a retired manufacturer of painting materials, informs Holmes that he had married a woman twenty years younger than himself, and that she had become intimate with his chess-playing acquaintance, Dr Ray Ernest. Mrs Amberley had

THE STRAND MAGAZINE, *January 1927, the New Year edition featuring the first British publication of* The Adventure of the Retired Colourman.

recently disappeared with Amberley's money. Watson is sent to investigate the affair, but notes nothing unusual except a strong smell of paint in the house. Amberley visits Holmes again, having received a telegram summoning him to a small village in Essex. Watson and Amberley travel to the village and find that the telegram was a hoax. When they return the next day, Holmes accuses Amberley of murdering his wife and her suspected lover. Amberley fails to kill himself and is arrested.

THE STRAND MAGAZINE, *January 1927, the New Year edition featuring the first British publication of* The Adventure of the Retired Colourman.

Holmes visits Amberley's house with Inspector McKinnon the next day and explains that he had diverted Amberley to Essex in order to search Amberley's house. He had found a gas-pipe leading into a gas-tight room, where he had found the start of a note written low down on a wall, and had deduced that Amberley had gassed the lovers and then disposed of the bodies. The fresh paint had been used to hide the residual smell of the gas. The bodies are later found in a disused well.

This case contains an example of a problem which must have occurred several times in the course of Holmes's career. He hands over the glory for solving the case to Inspector McKinnon, but then mentions that Watson might be able to write up the case later. Such an account, as this particular one demonstrates, would inevitably reveal that the police did not deserve the credit for solving the case. There is a problem when Holmes suggests that a pencil might later be found on one of the bodies. Anyone who had become unconscious in the middle of writing a sentence would either have the pencil in their hand, where Amberley would almost certainly have seen it, or else it would have dropped onto the floor, where Amberley or Holmes would have found it. The writer would certainly not have replaced it in his pocket.

THE ADVENTURE OF THE VEILED LODGER

First published: *Liberty* in January 1927
Main Characters: Mrs Merrilow, Eugenia Ronder, Mr Ronder, Leonardo

Mrs Merrilow, a landlady from South Brixton, informs Holmes that her solitary lodger, Eugenia Ronder, has a disfigured face which she keeps veiled. Her lodger has avoided society and has lately been disturbed by dreams involving murder and been heard shouting "coward" in her sleep.

Holmes recalls that the Ronders had been show-people and that an accident had occured seven years before wherein Mr Ronder had been killed by an escaped lion and Mrs Ronder badly mauled.

When Holmes and Watson visit Mrs Ronder she informs them that her husband had ill-treated her and that her lover, Leonardo, had killed Ronder with a club fitted with nails to simulate a lion's claw. When, as planned, Mrs Ronder freed the lion, it unexpectedly attacked her, and Leonardo fled in fear. As Leonardo had recently died, Eugenia wished to have the truth recorded before she might die. Holmes gently warns her against thoughts of suicide and she accepts his advice.

This is the shortest of the Holmes narratives, occupying less than six pages of text when later published in *The Strand Maga-*zine, but it includes an important point. The seventeen years of collaboration mentioned by Watson must be fitted between 1881, when they met, and 1903. In addition to the missing three years after Reichenbach there are two years unaccounted for, which can be explained by means of a misreading of a doctor's "19" as a "17", or by Watson being absent on Army medical duties during some of the Canonically non-busy years of the Boer Wars. Holmes's more sympathetic side is well demonstrated in the advice which he gives to Eugenia, and in the pride which he takes in her response.

THE ADVENTURE OF SHOSCOMBE OLD PLACE

First published: *Liberty* in March 1927
Main Characters: Sir Robert Norberton, Lady Beatrice Falder, John Mason, "Shoscombe Prince"

Holmes asks for information on Sir Robert Norberton, and Watson recalls that Sir Robert had once horse-whipped a money-lender, and that his home at Shoscombe Old Place is his racehorse training centre. The house is owned by his widowed sister, Lady Beatrice Falder, who also lives there and who breeds spaniels.

Norberton's head trainer, John Mason, visits 221B and reports that he considers Sir Robert to have gone mad, partly from the strain of knowing that his fate depends entirely on his horse, Shoscombe Prince, winning the Derby. Norberton had recently given Lady Beatrice's favourite spaniel away for no apparent reason, and had been meeting a mysterious man in the crypt of the old church. Lady Beatrice, too, appears to have changed her character. Mason had now found some ancient human remains in the crypt.

Holmes and Watson travel to Shoscombe, supposedly on a fishing trip. The next day they borrow Lady Beatrice's favourite spaniel from its new owner, the local publican, for a walk. The dog runs to Lady Beatrice's carriage but snaps at the lady inside. When Holmes visits the crypt he finds, as he expected, that the remains have gone, and as he opens one of the tombs he is interrupted by Sir Robert's arrival. Norberton admits that the tomb contains Lady Beatrice's body, as she had died a week previously of natural causes. If the death had been announced at the time, Norberton would have lost his horse to the money-lender he had once attacked. The husband of Lady Beatrice's maid had been impersonating Lady Beatrice until the race, when she would have been given a proper burial. Shoscombe Prince does win the Derby and Sir Robert re-establishes himself.

It is strange that the last case which was recorded about Holmes's exploits should be one of those in which no serious crime is actually committed. There is a nice touch of character in connection with Watson's admission that he loses half of his wound pension on horseracing. A less endearing trait is revealed when Watson finds it difficult to accept that a member of the minor nobility might have murdered his own sister, considering all the previous experiences with the nobility which Watson had recorded. It appears that Watson still would not learn from experience, but then, as Holmes states in the chronologically last case of their adventures together, *His Last Bow*, Watson never changes.

DR JOSEPH BELL *(above),*
Conan Doyle's tutor at
Edinburgh University, whose
exceptional powers of
observation were, in part, the
inspiration for Sherlock
Holmes.

LOUISA HAWKINS *("Touie")*
(above right), Conan Doyle's
first wife, who died on
4th July 1906, was a sister of
one of his patients. Touie was
very supportive of Doyle's
earlier literary efforts.

Doyle that the novel became a topic of conversation between himself and Oscar Wilde when the two met, along with J.M. Stoddart of *Lippincott's Monthly Magazine* for a dinner in the summer of 1889; a dinner which ended with Conan Doyle receiving a commission to write a further Sherlock Holmes adventure (*The Sign of the Four*), and Wilde the commission for *The Picture of Dorian Gray.*

Meanwhile, other events had occurred in Conan Doyle's life which were to influence his actions and beliefs for many years to come. In 1885, he married Louise Hawkins ("Touie") whose constant poor health was to lead to frequent domestic upheaval in the forthcoming years, and in 1886 he began to develop an interest in psychic studies following meetings which he had attended in Southsea.

By 1890, Conan Doyle had resolved that a change was necessary and that he would journey to Vienna to study the eye. By the spring of 1891, the Doyles were back in London, renting rooms in Montague Place whilst Conan Doyle looked around for a suitable office to put up his plate as an oculist. He eventually found accommodation at 2 Devonshire Place. The patients did not come, however, and, without even a ring at the doorbell to disturb him, he was able to devote his time to writing.

It was fortuitous that *The Strand Magazine* first saw publication about this time, in January 1891, and that Conan Doyle took the opportunity on hand to revive the Sherlock Holmes of his two successful novels for a series of adventures. *A Scandal in Bohemia* was the first to appear, in July 1891. Doyle continued to contribute adventures featuring Sherlock Holmes to *The Strand Magazine* but nonetheless, while he was writing these Holmes stories, he was anxious that he should be writing books that would make his a "lasting name in English literature". In November 1891, he wrote to his mother: "I think of slaying Holmes . . . and winding him up for good and all. He takes my mind from better things."

The idea of Holmes's death remained with him, and it seems that it was during a visit to Switzerland in 1893 that Doyle was shown the Reichenbach Falls, which he was subsequently to choose as the location for the "fatal" struggle with Moriarty. *The Final Problem*, the adventure which was to bring the news of Sherlock Holmes's death to a horrified nation, appeared in *The Strand Magazine* in December 1893. It is with the apparent death of the great detective that we can best leave the relationship between Conan Doyle and Holmes in order to concentrate on the many other varied events which filled Conan Doyle's life.

The tuberculosis to which Touie had become prey had completely disorganized the lives of the couple, and it was hoped that a winter in Egypt might effect a cure. The Doyles left England in the autumn of 1895 and journeyed to Cairo. The surroundings were to provide Conan Doyle with his plot

THE STRAND MAGAZINE, *July 1891, containing* A Scandal in Bohemia, *the first Sherlock Holmes short story and the first to be illustrated by Sidney Paget (left).*

for the desert drama *The Tragedy of the Korosko*, which first appeared in 1898. It was during this visit to Egypt that fighting broke out between the British and the Dervishes, and Conan Doyle seized the opportunity which presented itself to cable *The Westminster Gazette* asking to be appointed their honorary war correspondent. In this capacity he made his way to the front to witness the action at first hand: an experience which would equip him well for similar involvement in war, and war reporting, in later years.

Shortly after their return to England, the Doyles moved into a new house which Sir Arthur had had built at Hindhead in Surrey – an area chosen because it was believed that the air of the Surrey countryside would be beneficial to the health of the ailing Touie. Meanwhile, Conan Doyle's literary output continued unabated and, during this period, he produced his famous novel of the Regency, *Rodney Stone*; a tale of early married life, *A Duet with an Occasional Chorus*; and his Napoleonic portrait, *Uncle Bernac*.

In late December 1899, Conan Doyle once more became involved with warfare as the shadow of the problems in South Africa

CONAN DOYLE *demonstrating his Norwegian skis at Davos Platz in 1894, The first time that such skis were introduced to Switzerland (left below).*

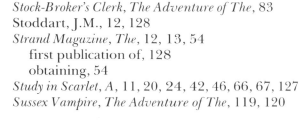

ACKNOWLEDGEMENTS

British Telecom's permanent exhibition *The Story of Telecommunications*: 27 above; 28. Richard Lancelyn Green: 8; 11 left; 13 left, above; 14 far right; 15 left above; 16 right above, below, right; 17 below (courtesy ITC/Rank), far left; 18; 21 above; 29; 30; 32; 37; 38; 40 above centre (courtesy ITC/Rank), above right, below; 42 left, right; 43 above left; 45; 48; 50; 53; 55 left, above; 60; 61 left; 62; 65 left; 68 below; 69 left; 70 below; 71–88; 89 above, left; 90; 91 far left, left; 92; 95–97; 99; 101–109; 113; 114; 118; 125; 126; 127 above; 129 left below; 130 top; 131–136; 137 below. Stanley MacKenzie: 6; 10; 11 above; 12; 14 right, above; 15 above, left below; 16 above; 17 left; 19; 20 below; 25 below; 27 left; 31 below, left; 34; 36 below; 39 left; 40 left; 41; 42 below; 43 above right; 51 right, left, below; 52; 54; 55 left; 56; 57; 58 right, far right, below; 59 far left, left, near left; 60 right, right above; 64; 65 far left, below; 66; 67; 69 above; 89 far left; 90; 91 above, left below; 94; 99; 110; 111; 116; 120; 127 right; 128; 129 left; 130 above; 137 above. Metropolitan Police Museum: 23; 24; 25 right below, left below, above; 26; 46. National Portrait Gallery, London: 122. Sherlock Holmes Pub: 20 above; 21 left; 22; 35 left, above; 70 far right; 93. Philip Weller: 7; 21 left above; 36 above left, above; 39 above; 43 above; 58 right; 59 second row from top; 60 near right, top left, second row left, centre; 61 below; 68 above.

Special photography Andy Stewart.